PASSWORD ORGANIZER

This Log Book Belongs To:

By: Beth L. Wickstrum

HomeTrees Press
Ojai • California

PASSWORD ORGANIZER

Website Name:

Web Address: ____________________

Login/Username: ____________________

Email: ____________________

Password: ____________________

New Password: ____________________ Date Changed: __________

New Password: ____________________ Date Changed: __________

New Password: ____________________ Date Changed: __________

Security Question Answer 1: ____________________

Security Question Answer 2: ____________________

Security Question Answer 3: ____________________

Website Name:

Web Address: ____________________

Login/Username: ____________________

Email: ____________________

Password: ____________________

New Password: ____________________ Date Changed: __________

New Password: ____________________ Date Changed: __________

New Password: ____________________ Date Changed: __________

Security Question Answer 1: ____________________

Security Question Answer 2: ____________________

Security Question Answer 3: ____________________

Website Name:

Web Address: ____________________

Login/Username: ____________________

Email: ____________________

Password: ____________________

New Password: ____________________ Date Changed: __________

New Password: ____________________ Date Changed: __________

New Password: ____________________ Date Changed: __________

Security Question Answer 1: ____________________

Security Question Answer 2: ____________________

Security Question Answer 3: ____________________

Website Name:

Web Address: ____________________

Login/Username: ____________________

Email: ____________________

Password: ____________________

New Password: ____________________ Date Changed: __________

New Password: ____________________ Date Changed: __________

New Password: ____________________ Date Changed: __________

Security Question Answer 1: ____________________

Security Question Answer 2: ____________________

Security Question Answer 3: ____________________

Website Name:

Web Address: ____________________

Login/Username: ____________________

Email: ____________________

Password: ____________________

New Password: ____________________ Date Changed: __________

New Password: ____________________ Date Changed: __________

New Password: ____________________ Date Changed: __________

Security Question Answer 1: ____________________

Security Question Answer 2: ____________________

Security Question Answer 3: ____________________

Website Name:

Web Address: ____________________

Login/Username: ____________________

Email: ____________________

Password: ____________________

New Password: ____________________ Date Changed: __________

New Password: ____________________ Date Changed: __________

New Password: ____________________ Date Changed: __________

Security Question Answer 1: ____________________

Security Question Answer 2: ____________________

Security Question Answer 3: ____________________

PASSWORD ORGANIZER

Website Name:

Web Address: ______
Login/Username: ______
Email: ______
Password: ______
New Password: ______ Date Changed: ______
New Password: ______ Date Changed: ______
New Password: ______ Date Changed: ______
Security Question Answer 1: ______
Security Question Answer 2: ______
Security Question Answer 3: ______

Website Name:

Web Address: ______
Login/Username: ______
Email: ______
Password: ______
New Password: ______ Date Changed: ______
New Password: ______ Date Changed: ______
New Password: ______ Date Changed: ______
Security Question Answer 1: ______
Security Question Answer 2: ______
Security Question Answer 3: ______

Website Name:

Web Address: ______
Login/Username: ______
Email: ______
Password: ______
New Password: ______ Date Changed: ______
New Password: ______ Date Changed: ______
New Password: ______ Date Changed: ______
Security Question Answer 1: ______
Security Question Answer 2: ______
Security Question Answer 3: ______

Website Name:

Web Address: ______

Login/Username: ______

Email: ______

Password: ______

New Password: ______ Date Changed: ______

New Password: ______ Date Changed: ______

New Password: ______ Date Changed: ______

Security Question Answer 1: ______

Security Question Answer 2: ______

Security Question Answer 3: ______

Website Name:

Web Address: ______

Login/Username: ______

Email: ______

Password: ______

New Password: ______ Date Changed: ______

New Password: ______ Date Changed: ______

New Password: ______ Date Changed: ______

Security Question Answer 1: ______

Security Question Answer 2: ______

Security Question Answer 3: ______

Website Name:

Web Address: ______

Login/Username: ______

Email: ______

Password: ______

New Password: ______ Date Changed: ______

New Password: ______ Date Changed: ______

New Password: ______ Date Changed: ______

Security Question Answer 1: ______

Security Question Answer 2: ______

Security Question Answer 3: ______

PASSWORD ORGANIZER

Website Name:

Web Address: ____________________
Login/Username: ____________________
Email: ____________________
Password: ____________________
New Password: ____________________ Date Changed: __________
New Password: ____________________ Date Changed: __________
New Password: ____________________ Date Changed: __________
Security Question Answer 1: ____________________
Security Question Answer 2: ____________________
Security Question Answer 3: ____________________

Website Name:

Web Address: ____________________
Login/Username: ____________________
Email: ____________________
Password: ____________________
New Password: ____________________ Date Changed: __________
New Password: ____________________ Date Changed: __________
New Password: ____________________ Date Changed: __________
Security Question Answer 1: ____________________
Security Question Answer 2: ____________________
Security Question Answer 3: ____________________

Website Name:

Web Address: ____________________
Login/Username: ____________________
Email: ____________________
Password: ____________________
New Password: ____________________ Date Changed: __________
New Password: ____________________ Date Changed: __________
New Password: ____________________ Date Changed: __________
Security Question Answer 1: ____________________
Security Question Answer 2: ____________________
Security Question Answer 3: ____________________

PASSWORD ORGANIZER

B

Website Name:

Web Address: ______________________

Login/Username: ______________________

Email: ______________________

Password: ______________________

New Password: ______________________ Date Changed: __________

New Password: ______________________ Date Changed: __________

New Password: ______________________ Date Changed: __________

Security Question Answer 1: ______________________

Security Question Answer 2: ______________________

Security Question Answer 3: ______________________

Website Name:

Web Address: ______________________

Login/Username: ______________________

Email: ______________________

Password: ______________________

New Password: ______________________ Date Changed: __________

New Password: ______________________ Date Changed: __________

New Password: ______________________ Date Changed: __________

Security Question Answer 1: ______________________

Security Question Answer 2: ______________________

Security Question Answer 3: ______________________

Website Name:

Web Address: ______________________

Login/Username: ______________________

Email: ______________________

Password: ______________________

New Password: ______________________ Date Changed: __________

New Password: ______________________ Date Changed: __________

New Password: ______________________ Date Changed: __________

Security Question Answer 1: ______________________

Security Question Answer 2: ______________________

Security Question Answer 3: ______________________

PASSWORD ORGANIZER

Website Name:

Web Address: ______________________

Login/Username: ______________________

Email: ______________________

Password: ______________________

New Password: ______________________ Date Changed: __________

New Password: ______________________ Date Changed: __________

New Password: ______________________ Date Changed: __________

Security Question Answer 1: ______________________

Security Question Answer 2: ______________________

Security Question Answer 3: ______________________

Website Name:

Web Address: ______________________

Login/Username: ______________________

Email: ______________________

Password: ______________________

New Password: ______________________ Date Changed: __________

New Password: ______________________ Date Changed: __________

New Password: ______________________ Date Changed: __________

Security Question Answer 1: ______________________

Security Question Answer 2: ______________________

Security Question Answer 3: ______________________

Website Name:

Web Address: ______________________

Login/Username: ______________________

Email: ______________________

Password: ______________________

New Password: ______________________ Date Changed: __________

New Password: ______________________ Date Changed: __________

New Password: ______________________ Date Changed: __________

Security Question Answer 1: ______________________

Security Question Answer 2: ______________________

Security Question Answer 3: ______________________

Website Name:

Web Address: __________

Login/Username: __________

Email: __________

Password: __________

New Password: __________ Date Changed: __________

New Password: __________ Date Changed: __________

New Password: __________ Date Changed: __________

Security Question Answer 1: __________

Security Question Answer 2: __________

Security Question Answer 3: __________

Website Name:

Web Address: __________

Login/Username: __________

Email: __________

Password: __________

New Password: __________ Date Changed: __________

New Password: __________ Date Changed: __________

New Password: __________ Date Changed: __________

Security Question Answer 1: __________

Security Question Answer 2: __________

Security Question Answer 3: __________

Website Name:

Web Address: __________

Login/Username: __________

Email: __________

Password: __________

New Password: __________ Date Changed: __________

New Password: __________ Date Changed: __________

New Password: __________ Date Changed: __________

Security Question Answer 1: __________

Security Question Answer 2: __________

Security Question Answer 3: __________

PASSWORD ORGANIZER

Website Name:

Web Address: ______
Login/Username: ______
Email: ______
Password: ______
New Password: ______ Date Changed: ______
New Password: ______ Date Changed: ______
New Password: ______ Date Changed: ______
Security Question Answer 1: ______
Security Question Answer 2: ______
Security Question Answer 3: ______

Website Name:

Web Address: ______
Login/Username: ______
Email: ______
Password: ______
New Password: ______ Date Changed: ______
New Password: ______ Date Changed: ______
New Password: ______ Date Changed: ______
Security Question Answer 1: ______
Security Question Answer 2: ______
Security Question Answer 3: ______

Website Name:

Web Address: ______
Login/Username: ______
Email: ______
Password: ______
New Password: ______ Date Changed: ______
New Password: ______ Date Changed: ______
New Password: ______ Date Changed: ______
Security Question Answer 1: ______
Security Question Answer 2: ______
Security Question Answer 3: ______

Website Name:

Web Address: ______________________
Login/Username: ______________________
Email: ______________________
Password: ______________________
New Password: ______________________ Date Changed: __________
New Password: ______________________ Date Changed: __________
New Password: ______________________ Date Changed: __________
Security Question Answer 1: ______________________
Security Question Answer 2: ______________________
Security Question Answer 3: ______________________

Website Name:

Web Address: ______________________
Login/Username: ______________________
Email: ______________________
Password: ______________________
New Password: ______________________ Date Changed: __________
New Password: ______________________ Date Changed: __________
New Password: ______________________ Date Changed: __________
Security Question Answer 1: ______________________
Security Question Answer 2: ______________________
Security Question Answer 3: ______________________

Website Name:

Web Address: ______________________
Login/Username: ______________________
Email: ______________________
Password: ______________________
New Password: ______________________ Date Changed: __________
New Password: ______________________ Date Changed: __________
New Password: ______________________ Date Changed: __________
Security Question Answer 1: ______________________
Security Question Answer 2: ______________________
Security Question Answer 3: ______________________

PASSWORD ORGANIZER

Website Name:

Web Address: ____________________
Login/Username: ____________________
Email: ____________________
Password: ____________________
New Password: ____________________ Date Changed: __________
New Password: ____________________ Date Changed: __________
New Password: ____________________ Date Changed: __________
Security Question Answer 1: ____________________
Security Question Answer 2: ____________________
Security Question Answer 3: ____________________

Website Name:

Web Address: ____________________
Login/Username: ____________________
Email: ____________________
Password: ____________________
New Password: ____________________ Date Changed: __________
New Password: ____________________ Date Changed: __________
New Password: ____________________ Date Changed: __________
Security Question Answer 1: ____________________
Security Question Answer 2: ____________________
Security Question Answer 3: ____________________

Website Name:

Web Address: ____________________
Login/Username: ____________________
Email: ____________________
Password: ____________________
New Password: ____________________ Date Changed: __________
New Password: ____________________ Date Changed: __________
New Password: ____________________ Date Changed: __________
Security Question Answer 1: ____________________
Security Question Answer 2: ____________________
Security Question Answer 3: ____________________

Website Name:

Web Address: ______

Login/Username: ______

Email: ______

Password: ______

New Password: ______ Date Changed: ______

New Password: ______ Date Changed: ______

New Password: ______ Date Changed: ______

Security Question Answer 1: ______

Security Question Answer 2: ______

Security Question Answer 3: ______

Website Name:

Web Address: ______

Login/Username: ______

Email: ______

Password: ______

New Password: ______ Date Changed: ______

New Password: ______ Date Changed: ______

New Password: ______ Date Changed: ______

Security Question Answer 1: ______

Security Question Answer 2: ______

Security Question Answer 3: ______

Website Name:

Web Address: ______

Login/Username: ______

Email: ______

Password: ______

New Password: ______ Date Changed: ______

New Password: ______ Date Changed: ______

New Password: ______ Date Changed: ______

Security Question Answer 1: ______

Security Question Answer 2: ______

Security Question Answer 3: ______

PASSWORD ORGANIZER

Website Name:

Web Address: __________
Login/Username: __________
Email: __________
Password: __________
New Password: __________ Date Changed: __________
New Password: __________ Date Changed: __________
New Password: __________ Date Changed: __________
Security Question Answer 1: __________
Security Question Answer 2: __________
Security Question Answer 3: __________

Website Name:

Web Address: __________
Login/Username: __________
Email: __________
Password: __________
New Password: __________ Date Changed: __________
New Password: __________ Date Changed: __________
New Password: __________ Date Changed: __________
Security Question Answer 1: __________
Security Question Answer 2: __________
Security Question Answer 3: __________

Website Name:

Web Address: __________
Login/Username: __________
Email: __________
Password: __________
New Password: __________ Date Changed: __________
New Password: __________ Date Changed: __________
New Password: __________ Date Changed: __________
Security Question Answer 1: __________
Security Question Answer 2: __________
Security Question Answer 3: __________

Website Name:

Web Address: ______

Login/Username: ______

Email: ______

Password: ______

New Password: ______ Date Changed: ______

New Password: ______ Date Changed: ______

New Password: ______ Date Changed: ______

Security Question Answer 1: ______

Security Question Answer 2: ______

Security Question Answer 3: ______

Website Name:

Web Address: ______

Login/Username: ______

Email: ______

Password: ______

New Password: ______ Date Changed: ______

New Password: ______ Date Changed: ______

New Password: ______ Date Changed: ______

Security Question Answer 1: ______

Security Question Answer 2: ______

Security Question Answer 3: ______

Website Name:

Web Address: ______

Login/Username: ______

Email: ______

Password: ______

New Password: ______ Date Changed: ______

New Password: ______ Date Changed: ______

New Password: ______ Date Changed: ______

Security Question Answer 1: ______

Security Question Answer 2: ______

Security Question Answer 3: ______

PASSWORD ORGANIZER

Website Name:

Web Address: ______________________________
Login/Username: ______________________________
Email: ______________________________
Password: ______________________________
New Password: ____________________ Date Changed: __________
New Password: ____________________ Date Changed: __________
New Password: ____________________ Date Changed: __________
Security Question Answer 1: ______________________________
Security Question Answer 2: ______________________________
Security Question Answer 3: ______________________________

Website Name:

Web Address: ______________________________
Login/Username: ______________________________
Email: ______________________________
Password: ______________________________
New Password: ____________________ Date Changed: __________
New Password: ____________________ Date Changed: __________
New Password: ____________________ Date Changed: __________
Security Question Answer 1: ______________________________
Security Question Answer 2: ______________________________
Security Question Answer 3: ______________________________

Website Name:

Web Address: ______________________________
Login/Username: ______________________________
Email: ______________________________
Password: ______________________________
New Password: ____________________ Date Changed: __________
New Password: ____________________ Date Changed: __________
New Password: ____________________ Date Changed: __________
Security Question Answer 1: ______________________________
Security Question Answer 2: ______________________________
Security Question Answer 3: ______________________________

Website Name:

Web Address: ______

Login/Username: ______

Email: ______

Password: ______

New Password: ______ Date Changed: ______

New Password: ______ Date Changed: ______

New Password: ______ Date Changed: ______

Security Question Answer 1: ______

Security Question Answer 2: ______

Security Question Answer 3: ______

Website Name:

Web Address: ______

Login/Username: ______

Email: ______

Password: ______

New Password: ______ Date Changed: ______

New Password: ______ Date Changed: ______

New Password: ______ Date Changed: ______

Security Question Answer 1: ______

Security Question Answer 2: ______

Security Question Answer 3: ______

Website Name:

Web Address: ______

Login/Username: ______

Email: ______

Password: ______

New Password: ______ Date Changed: ______

New Password: ______ Date Changed: ______

New Password: ______ Date Changed: ______

Security Question Answer 1: ______

Security Question Answer 2: ______

Security Question Answer 3: ______

PASSWORD ORGANIZER

Website Name:

Web Address: ______

Login/Username: ______

Email: ______

Password: ______

New Password: ______ Date Changed: ______

New Password: ______ Date Changed: ______

New Password: ______ Date Changed: ______

Security Question Answer 1: ______

Security Question Answer 2: ______

Security Question Answer 3: ______

Website Name:

Web Address: ______

Login/Username: ______

Email: ______

Password: ______

New Password: ______ Date Changed: ______

New Password: ______ Date Changed: ______

New Password: ______ Date Changed: ______

Security Question Answer 1: ______

Security Question Answer 2: ______

Security Question Answer 3: ______

Website Name:

Web Address: ______

Login/Username: ______

Email: ______

Password: ______

New Password: ______ Date Changed: ______

New Password: ______ Date Changed: ______

New Password: ______ Date Changed: ______

Security Question Answer 1: ______

Security Question Answer 2: ______

Security Question Answer 3: ______

PASSWORD ORGANIZER

Website Name:

Web Address: ____

Login/Username: ____

Email: ____

Password: ____

New Password: ____ Date Changed: ____

New Password: ____ Date Changed: ____

New Password: ____ Date Changed: ____

Security Question Answer 1: ____

Security Question Answer 2: ____

Security Question Answer 3: ____

Website Name:

Web Address: ____

Login/Username: ____

Email: ____

Password: ____

New Password: ____ Date Changed: ____

New Password: ____ Date Changed: ____

New Password: ____ Date Changed: ____

Security Question Answer 1: ____

Security Question Answer 2: ____

Security Question Answer 3: ____

Website Name:

Web Address: ____

Login/Username: ____

Email: ____

Password: ____

New Password: ____ Date Changed: ____

New Password: ____ Date Changed: ____

New Password: ____ Date Changed: ____

Security Question Answer 1: ____

Security Question Answer 2: ____

Security Question Answer 3: ____

PASSWORD ORGANIZER

Website Name:

Web Address: ____

Login/Username: ____

Email: ____

Password: ____

New Password: ____ Date Changed: ____

New Password: ____ Date Changed: ____

New Password: ____ Date Changed: ____

Security Question Answer 1: ____

Security Question Answer 2: ____

Security Question Answer 3: ____

Website Name:

Web Address: ____

Login/Username: ____

Email: ____

Password: ____

New Password: ____ Date Changed: ____

New Password: ____ Date Changed: ____

New Password: ____ Date Changed: ____

Security Question Answer 1: ____

Security Question Answer 2: ____

Security Question Answer 3: ____

Website Name:

Web Address: ____

Login/Username: ____

Email: ____

Password: ____

New Password: ____ Date Changed: ____

New Password: ____ Date Changed: ____

New Password: ____ Date Changed: ____

Security Question Answer 1: ____

Security Question Answer 2: ____

Security Question Answer 3: ____

Website Name:

Web Address: ______

Login/Username: ______

Email: ______

Password: ______

New Password: ______ Date Changed: ______

New Password: ______ Date Changed: ______

New Password: ______ Date Changed: ______

Security Question Answer 1: ______

Security Question Answer 2: ______

Security Question Answer 3: ______

Website Name:

Web Address: ______

Login/Username: ______

Email: ______

Password: ______

New Password: ______ Date Changed: ______

New Password: ______ Date Changed: ______

New Password: ______ Date Changed: ______

Security Question Answer 1: ______

Security Question Answer 2: ______

Security Question Answer 3: ______

Website Name:

Web Address: ______

Login/Username: ______

Email: ______

Password: ______

New Password: ______ Date Changed: ______

New Password: ______ Date Changed: ______

New Password: ______ Date Changed: ______

Security Question Answer 1: ______

Security Question Answer 2: ______

Security Question Answer 3: ______

PASSWORD ORGANIZER

Website Name:

Web Address: ______

Login/Username: ______

Email: ______

Password: ______

New Password: ______ Date Changed: ______

New Password: ______ Date Changed: ______

New Password: ______ Date Changed: ______

Security Question Answer 1: ______

Security Question Answer 2: ______

Security Question Answer 3: ______

Website Name:

Web Address: ______

Login/Username: ______

Email: ______

Password: ______

New Password: ______ Date Changed: ______

New Password: ______ Date Changed: ______

New Password: ______ Date Changed: ______

Security Question Answer 1: ______

Security Question Answer 2: ______

Security Question Answer 3: ______

Website Name:

Web Address: ______

Login/Username: ______

Email: ______

Password: ______

New Password: ______ Date Changed: ______

New Password: ______ Date Changed: ______

New Password: ______ Date Changed: ______

Security Question Answer 1: ______

Security Question Answer 2: ______

Security Question Answer 3: ______

Website Name:

Web Address: ______

Login/Username: ______

Email: ______

Password: ______

New Password: ______ Date Changed: ______

New Password: ______ Date Changed: ______

New Password: ______ Date Changed: ______

Security Question Answer 1: ______

Security Question Answer 2: ______

Security Question Answer 3: ______

Website Name:

Web Address: ______

Login/Username: ______

Email: ______

Password: ______

New Password: ______ Date Changed: ______

New Password: ______ Date Changed: ______

New Password: ______ Date Changed: ______

Security Question Answer 1: ______

Security Question Answer 2: ______

Security Question Answer 3: ______

Website Name:

Web Address: ______

Login/Username: ______

Email: ______

Password: ______

New Password: ______ Date Changed: ______

New Password: ______ Date Changed: ______

New Password: ______ Date Changed: ______

Security Question Answer 1: ______

Security Question Answer 2: ______

Security Question Answer 3: ______

PASSWORD ORGANIZER

Website Name:

Web Address: ____________________

Login/Username: ____________________

Email: ____________________

Password: ____________________

New Password: ____________________ Date Changed: __________

New Password: ____________________ Date Changed: __________

New Password: ____________________ Date Changed: __________

Security Question Answer 1: ____________________

Security Question Answer 2: ____________________

Security Question Answer 3: ____________________

Website Name:

Web Address: ____________________

Login/Username: ____________________

Email: ____________________

Password: ____________________

New Password: ____________________ Date Changed: __________

New Password: ____________________ Date Changed: __________

New Password: ____________________ Date Changed: __________

Security Question Answer 1: ____________________

Security Question Answer 2: ____________________

Security Question Answer 3: ____________________

Website Name:

Web Address: ____________________

Login/Username: ____________________

Email: ____________________

Password: ____________________

New Password: ____________________ Date Changed: __________

New Password: ____________________ Date Changed: __________

New Password: ____________________ Date Changed: __________

Security Question Answer 1: ____________________

Security Question Answer 2: ____________________

Security Question Answer 3: ____________________

Website Name:

Web Address: ____________________

Login/Username: ____________________

Email: ____________________

Password: ____________________

New Password: ____________________ Date Changed: __________

New Password: ____________________ Date Changed: __________

New Password: ____________________ Date Changed: __________

Security Question Answer 1: ____________________

Security Question Answer 2: ____________________

Security Question Answer 3: ____________________

Website Name:

Web Address: ____________________

Login/Username: ____________________

Email: ____________________

Password: ____________________

New Password: ____________________ Date Changed: __________

New Password: ____________________ Date Changed: __________

New Password: ____________________ Date Changed: __________

Security Question Answer 1: ____________________

Security Question Answer 2: ____________________

Security Question Answer 3: ____________________

Website Name:

Web Address: ____________________

Login/Username: ____________________

Email: ____________________

Password: ____________________

New Password: ____________________ Date Changed: __________

New Password: ____________________ Date Changed: __________

New Password: ____________________ Date Changed: __________

Security Question Answer 1: ____________________

Security Question Answer 2: ____________________

Security Question Answer 3: ____________________

PASSWORD ORGANIZER

Website Name:

Web Address: ________________

Login/Username: ________________

Email: ________________

Password: ________________

New Password: ________ Date Changed: ________

New Password: ________ Date Changed: ________

New Password: ________ Date Changed: ________

Security Question Answer 1: ________________

Security Question Answer 2: ________________

Security Question Answer 3: ________________

Website Name:

Web Address: ________________

Login/Username: ________________

Email: ________________

Password: ________________

New Password: ________ Date Changed: ________

New Password: ________ Date Changed: ________

New Password: ________ Date Changed: ________

Security Question Answer 1: ________________

Security Question Answer 2: ________________

Security Question Answer 3: ________________

Website Name:

Web Address: ________________

Login/Username: ________________

Email: ________________

Password: ________________

New Password: ________ Date Changed: ________

New Password: ________ Date Changed: ________

New Password: ________ Date Changed: ________

Security Question Answer 1: ________________

Security Question Answer 2: ________________

Security Question Answer 3: ________________

Website Name:

Web Address: ______

Login/Username: ______

Email: ______

Password: ______

New Password: ______ Date Changed: ______

New Password: ______ Date Changed: ______

New Password: ______ Date Changed: ______

Security Question Answer 1: ______

Security Question Answer 2: ______

Security Question Answer 3: ______

Website Name:

Web Address: ______

Login/Username: ______

Email: ______

Password: ______

New Password: ______ Date Changed: ______

New Password: ______ Date Changed: ______

New Password: ______ Date Changed: ______

Security Question Answer 1: ______

Security Question Answer 2: ______

Security Question Answer 3: ______

Website Name:

Web Address: ______

Login/Username: ______

Email: ______

Password: ______

New Password: ______ Date Changed: ______

New Password: ______ Date Changed: ______

New Password: ______ Date Changed: ______

Security Question Answer 1: ______

Security Question Answer 2: ______

Security Question Answer 3: ______

PASSWORD ORGANIZER

Website Name:

Web Address: ______________________________

Login/Username: ______________________________

Email: ______________________________

Password: ______________________________

New Password: ____________________ Date Changed: __________

New Password: ____________________ Date Changed: __________

New Password: ____________________ Date Changed: __________

Security Question Answer 1: ______________________________

Security Question Answer 2: ______________________________

Security Question Answer 3: ______________________________

Website Name:

Web Address: ______________________________

Login/Username: ______________________________

Email: ______________________________

Password: ______________________________

New Password: ____________________ Date Changed: __________

New Password: ____________________ Date Changed: __________

New Password: ____________________ Date Changed: __________

Security Question Answer 1: ______________________________

Security Question Answer 2: ______________________________

Security Question Answer 3: ______________________________

Website Name:

Web Address: ______________________________

Login/Username: ______________________________

Email: ______________________________

Password: ______________________________

New Password: ____________________ Date Changed: __________

New Password: ____________________ Date Changed: __________

New Password: ____________________ Date Changed: __________

Security Question Answer 1: ______________________________

Security Question Answer 2: ______________________________

Security Question Answer 3: ______________________________

Website Name:

Web Address: ____________________

Login/Username: ____________________

Email: ____________________

Password: ____________________

New Password: ____________________ Date Changed: __________

New Password: ____________________ Date Changed: __________

New Password: ____________________ Date Changed: __________

Security Question Answer 1: ____________________

Security Question Answer 2: ____________________

Security Question Answer 3: ____________________

Website Name:

Web Address: ____________________

Login/Username: ____________________

Email: ____________________

Password: ____________________

New Password: ____________________ Date Changed: __________

New Password: ____________________ Date Changed: __________

New Password: ____________________ Date Changed: __________

Security Question Answer 1: ____________________

Security Question Answer 2: ____________________

Security Question Answer 3: ____________________

Website Name:

Web Address: ____________________

Login/Username: ____________________

Email: ____________________

Password: ____________________

New Password: ____________________ Date Changed: __________

New Password: ____________________ Date Changed: __________

New Password: ____________________ Date Changed: __________

Security Question Answer 1: ____________________

Security Question Answer 2: ____________________

Security Question Answer 3: ____________________

PASSWORD ORGANIZER

Website Name:

Web Address: ______

Login/Username: ______

Email: ______

Password: ______

New Password: ______ Date Changed: ______

New Password: ______ Date Changed: ______

New Password: ______ Date Changed: ______

Security Question Answer 1: ______

Security Question Answer 2: ______

Security Question Answer 3: ______

Website Name:

Web Address: ______

Login/Username: ______

Email: ______

Password: ______

New Password: ______ Date Changed: ______

New Password: ______ Date Changed: ______

New Password: ______ Date Changed: ______

Security Question Answer 1: ______

Security Question Answer 2: ______

Security Question Answer 3: ______

Website Name:

Web Address: ______

Login/Username: ______

Email: ______

Password: ______

New Password: ______ Date Changed: ______

New Password: ______ Date Changed: ______

New Password: ______ Date Changed: ______

Security Question Answer 1: ______

Security Question Answer 2: ______

Security Question Answer 3: ______

Website Name:

Web Address: ______

Login/Username: ______

Email: ______

Password: ______

New Password: ______ Date Changed: ______

New Password: ______ Date Changed: ______

New Password: ______ Date Changed: ______

Security Question Answer 1: ______

Security Question Answer 2: ______

Security Question Answer 3: ______

Website Name:

Web Address: ______

Login/Username: ______

Email: ______

Password: ______

New Password: ______ Date Changed: ______

New Password: ______ Date Changed: ______

New Password: ______ Date Changed: ______

Security Question Answer 1: ______

Security Question Answer 2: ______

Security Question Answer 3: ______

Website Name:

Web Address: ______

Login/Username: ______

Email: ______

Password: ______

New Password: ______ Date Changed: ______

New Password: ______ Date Changed: ______

New Password: ______ Date Changed: ______

Security Question Answer 1: ______

Security Question Answer 2: ______

Security Question Answer 3: ______

PASSWORD ORGANIZER

Website Name:

Web Address: ___

Login/Username: ___

Email: ___

Password: ___

New Password: ___ Date Changed: ___

New Password: ___ Date Changed: ___

New Password: ___ Date Changed: ___

Security Question Answer 1: ___

Security Question Answer 2: ___

Security Question Answer 3: ___

Website Name:

Web Address: ___

Login/Username: ___

Email: ___

Password: ___

New Password: ___ Date Changed: ___

New Password: ___ Date Changed: ___

New Password: ___ Date Changed: ___

Security Question Answer 1: ___

Security Question Answer 2: ___

Security Question Answer 3: ___

Website Name:

Web Address: ___

Login/Username: ___

Email: ___

Password: ___

New Password: ___ Date Changed: ___

New Password: ___ Date Changed: ___

New Password: ___ Date Changed: ___

Security Question Answer 1: ___

Security Question Answer 2: ___

Security Question Answer 3: ___

PASSWORD ORGANIZER

Website Name:

Web Address: ______________________________

Login/Username: ______________________________

Email: ______________________________

Password: ______________________________

New Password: ____________________ Date Changed: __________

New Password: ____________________ Date Changed: __________

New Password: ____________________ Date Changed: __________

Security Question Answer 1: ______________________________

Security Question Answer 2: ______________________________

Security Question Answer 3: ______________________________

Website Name:

Web Address: ______________________________

Login/Username: ______________________________

Email: ______________________________

Password: ______________________________

New Password: ____________________ Date Changed: __________

New Password: ____________________ Date Changed: __________

New Password: ____________________ Date Changed: __________

Security Question Answer 1: ______________________________

Security Question Answer 2: ______________________________

Security Question Answer 3: ______________________________

Website Name:

Web Address: ______________________________

Login/Username: ______________________________

Email: ______________________________

Password: ______________________________

New Password: ____________________ Date Changed: __________

New Password: ____________________ Date Changed: __________

New Password: ____________________ Date Changed: __________

Security Question Answer 1: ______________________________

Security Question Answer 2: ______________________________

Security Question Answer 3: ______________________________

PASSWORD ORGANIZER

Website Name:

Web Address: ______________________
Login/Username: ______________________
Email: ______________________
Password: ______________________
New Password: ______________________ Date Changed: __________
New Password: ______________________ Date Changed: __________
New Password: ______________________ Date Changed: __________
Security Question Answer 1: ______________________
Security Question Answer 2: ______________________
Security Question Answer 3: ______________________

Website Name:

Web Address: ______________________
Login/Username: ______________________
Email: ______________________
Password: ______________________
New Password: ______________________ Date Changed: __________
New Password: ______________________ Date Changed: __________
New Password: ______________________ Date Changed: __________
Security Question Answer 1: ______________________
Security Question Answer 2: ______________________
Security Question Answer 3: ______________________

Website Name:

Web Address: ______________________
Login/Username: ______________________
Email: ______________________
Password: ______________________
New Password: ______________________ Date Changed: __________
New Password: ______________________ Date Changed: __________
New Password: ______________________ Date Changed: __________
Security Question Answer 1: ______________________
Security Question Answer 2: ______________________
Security Question Answer 3: ______________________

Website Name:

Web Address: ______

Login/Username: ______

Email: ______

Password: ______

New Password: ______ Date Changed: ______

New Password: ______ Date Changed: ______

New Password: ______ Date Changed: ______

Security Question Answer 1: ______

Security Question Answer 2: ______

Security Question Answer 3: ______

Website Name:

Web Address: ______

Login/Username: ______

Email: ______

Password: ______

New Password: ______ Date Changed: ______

New Password: ______ Date Changed: ______

New Password: ______ Date Changed: ______

Security Question Answer 1: ______

Security Question Answer 2: ______

Security Question Answer 3: ______

Website Name:

Web Address: ______

Login/Username: ______

Email: ______

Password: ______

New Password: ______ Date Changed: ______

New Password: ______ Date Changed: ______

New Password: ______ Date Changed: ______

Security Question Answer 1: ______

Security Question Answer 2: ______

Security Question Answer 3: ______

PASSWORD ORGANIZER

Website Name:

Web Address: ______________________________

Login/Username: ______________________________

Email: ______________________________

Password: ______________________________

New Password: ____________________ Date Changed: __________

New Password: ____________________ Date Changed: __________

New Password: ____________________ Date Changed: __________

Security Question Answer 1: ______________________________

Security Question Answer 2: ______________________________

Security Question Answer 3: ______________________________

Website Name:

Web Address: ______________________________

Login/Username: ______________________________

Email: ______________________________

Password: ______________________________

New Password: ____________________ Date Changed: __________

New Password: ____________________ Date Changed: __________

New Password: ____________________ Date Changed: __________

Security Question Answer 1: ______________________________

Security Question Answer 2: ______________________________

Security Question Answer 3: ______________________________

Website Name:

Web Address: ______________________________

Login/Username: ______________________________

Email: ______________________________

Password: ______________________________

New Password: ____________________ Date Changed: __________

New Password: ____________________ Date Changed: __________

New Password: ____________________ Date Changed: __________

Security Question Answer 1: ______________________________

Security Question Answer 2: ______________________________

Security Question Answer 3: ______________________________

Website Name:

Web Address: ____

Login/Username: ____

Email: ____

Password: ____

New Password: ____ Date Changed: ____

New Password: ____ Date Changed: ____

New Password: ____ Date Changed: ____

Security Question Answer 1: ____

Security Question Answer 2: ____

Security Question Answer 3: ____

Website Name:

Web Address: ____

Login/Username: ____

Email: ____

Password: ____

New Password: ____ Date Changed: ____

New Password: ____ Date Changed: ____

New Password: ____ Date Changed: ____

Security Question Answer 1: ____

Security Question Answer 2: ____

Security Question Answer 3: ____

Website Name:

Web Address: ____

Login/Username: ____

Email: ____

Password: ____

New Password: ____ Date Changed: ____

New Password: ____ Date Changed: ____

New Password: ____ Date Changed: ____

Security Question Answer 1: ____

Security Question Answer 2: ____

Security Question Answer 3: ____

PASSWORD ORGANIZER

Website Name:

Web Address: ____________________

Login/Username: ____________________

Email: ____________________

Password: ____________________

New Password: ____________________ Date Changed: __________

New Password: ____________________ Date Changed: __________

New Password: ____________________ Date Changed: __________

Security Question Answer 1: ____________________

Security Question Answer 2: ____________________

Security Question Answer 3: ____________________

Website Name:

Web Address: ____________________

Login/Username: ____________________

Email: ____________________

Password: ____________________

New Password: ____________________ Date Changed: __________

New Password: ____________________ Date Changed: __________

New Password: ____________________ Date Changed: __________

Security Question Answer 1: ____________________

Security Question Answer 2: ____________________

Security Question Answer 3: ____________________

Website Name:

Web Address: ____________________

Login/Username: ____________________

Email: ____________________

Password: ____________________

New Password: ____________________ Date Changed: __________

New Password: ____________________ Date Changed: __________

New Password: ____________________ Date Changed: __________

Security Question Answer 1: ____________________

Security Question Answer 2: ____________________

Security Question Answer 3: ____________________

Website Name:

Web Address: ______

Login/Username: ______

Email: ______

Password: ______

New Password: ______ Date Changed: ______

New Password: ______ Date Changed: ______

New Password: ______ Date Changed: ______

Security Question Answer 1: ______

Security Question Answer 2: ______

Security Question Answer 3: ______

Website Name:

Web Address: ______

Login/Username: ______

Email: ______

Password: ______

New Password: ______ Date Changed: ______

New Password: ______ Date Changed: ______

New Password: ______ Date Changed: ______

Security Question Answer 1: ______

Security Question Answer 2: ______

Security Question Answer 3: ______

Website Name:

Web Address: ______

Login/Username: ______

Email: ______

Password: ______

New Password: ______ Date Changed: ______

New Password: ______ Date Changed: ______

New Password: ______ Date Changed: ______

Security Question Answer 1: ______

Security Question Answer 2: ______

Security Question Answer 3: ______

PASSWORD ORGANIZER

Website Name:

Web Address: ____________________

Login/Username: ____________________

Email: ____________________

Password: ____________________

New Password: ____________________ Date Changed: __________

New Password: ____________________ Date Changed: __________

New Password: ____________________ Date Changed: __________

Security Question Answer 1: ____________________

Security Question Answer 2: ____________________

Security Question Answer 3: ____________________

Website Name:

Web Address: ____________________

Login/Username: ____________________

Email: ____________________

Password: ____________________

New Password: ____________________ Date Changed: __________

New Password: ____________________ Date Changed: __________

New Password: ____________________ Date Changed: __________

Security Question Answer 1: ____________________

Security Question Answer 2: ____________________

Security Question Answer 3: ____________________

Website Name:

Web Address: ____________________

Login/Username: ____________________

Email: ____________________

Password: ____________________

New Password: ____________________ Date Changed: __________

New Password: ____________________ Date Changed: __________

New Password: ____________________ Date Changed: __________

Security Question Answer 1: ____________________

Security Question Answer 2: ____________________

Security Question Answer 3: ____________________

Website Name:

Web Address: ______________________________

Login/Username: ______________________________

Email: ______________________________

Password: ______________________________

New Password: ______________________ Date Changed: __________

New Password: ______________________ Date Changed: __________

New Password: ______________________ Date Changed: __________

Security Question Answer 1: ______________________________

Security Question Answer 2: ______________________________

Security Question Answer 3: ______________________________

Website Name:

Web Address: ______________________________

Login/Username: ______________________________

Email: ______________________________

Password: ______________________________

New Password: ______________________ Date Changed: __________

New Password: ______________________ Date Changed: __________

New Password: ______________________ Date Changed: __________

Security Question Answer 1: ______________________________

Security Question Answer 2: ______________________________

Security Question Answer 3: ______________________________

Website Name:

Web Address: ______________________________

Login/Username: ______________________________

Email: ______________________________

Password: ______________________________

New Password: ______________________ Date Changed: __________

New Password: ______________________ Date Changed: __________

New Password: ______________________ Date Changed: __________

Security Question Answer 1: ______________________________

Security Question Answer 2: ______________________________

Security Question Answer 3: ______________________________

PASSWORD ORGANIZER

Website Name:

Web Address: ____________________

Login/Username: ____________________

Email: ____________________

Password: ____________________

New Password: ____________________ Date Changed: __________

New Password: ____________________ Date Changed: __________

New Password: ____________________ Date Changed: __________

Security Question Answer 1: ____________________

Security Question Answer 2: ____________________

Security Question Answer 3: ____________________

Website Name:

Web Address: ____________________

Login/Username: ____________________

Email: ____________________

Password: ____________________

New Password: ____________________ Date Changed: __________

New Password: ____________________ Date Changed: __________

New Password: ____________________ Date Changed: __________

Security Question Answer 1: ____________________

Security Question Answer 2: ____________________

Security Question Answer 3: ____________________

Website Name:

Web Address: ____________________

Login/Username: ____________________

Email: ____________________

Password: ____________________

New Password: ____________________ Date Changed: __________

New Password: ____________________ Date Changed: __________

New Password: ____________________ Date Changed: __________

Security Question Answer 1: ____________________

Security Question Answer 2: ____________________

Security Question Answer 3: ____________________

PASSWORD ORGANIZER

Website Name:

Web Address: ______________________

Login/Username: ______________________

Email: ______________________

Password: ______________________

New Password: ______________________ Date Changed: __________

New Password: ______________________ Date Changed: __________

New Password: ______________________ Date Changed: __________

Security Question Answer 1: ______________________

Security Question Answer 2: ______________________

Security Question Answer 3: ______________________

Website Name:

Web Address: ______________________

Login/Username: ______________________

Email: ______________________

Password: ______________________

New Password: ______________________ Date Changed: __________

New Password: ______________________ Date Changed: __________

New Password: ______________________ Date Changed: __________

Security Question Answer 1: ______________________

Security Question Answer 2: ______________________

Security Question Answer 3: ______________________

Website Name:

Web Address: ______________________

Login/Username: ______________________

Email: ______________________

Password: ______________________

New Password: ______________________ Date Changed: __________

New Password: ______________________ Date Changed: __________

New Password: ______________________ Date Changed: __________

Security Question Answer 1: ______________________

Security Question Answer 2: ______________________

Security Question Answer 3: ______________________

PASSWORD ORGANIZER

Website Name:

Web Address: __________
Login/Username: __________
Email: __________
Password: __________
New Password: __________ Date Changed: __________
New Password: __________ Date Changed: __________
New Password: __________ Date Changed: __________
Security Question Answer 1: __________
Security Question Answer 2: __________
Security Question Answer 3: __________

Website Name:

Web Address: __________
Login/Username: __________
Email: __________
Password: __________
New Password: __________ Date Changed: __________
New Password: __________ Date Changed: __________
New Password: __________ Date Changed: __________
Security Question Answer 1: __________
Security Question Answer 2: __________
Security Question Answer 3: __________

Website Name:

Web Address: __________
Login/Username: __________
Email: __________
Password: __________
New Password: __________ Date Changed: __________
New Password: __________ Date Changed: __________
New Password: __________ Date Changed: __________
Security Question Answer 1: __________
Security Question Answer 2: __________
Security Question Answer 3: __________

Website Name:

Web Address: ______

Login/Username: ______

Email: ______

Password: ______

New Password: ______ Date Changed: ______

New Password: ______ Date Changed: ______

New Password: ______ Date Changed: ______

Security Question Answer 1: ______

Security Question Answer 2: ______

Security Question Answer 3: ______

Website Name:

Web Address: ______

Login/Username: ______

Email: ______

Password: ______

New Password: ______ Date Changed: ______

New Password: ______ Date Changed: ______

New Password: ______ Date Changed: ______

Security Question Answer 1: ______

Security Question Answer 2: ______

Security Question Answer 3: ______

Website Name:

Web Address: ______

Login/Username: ______

Email: ______

Password: ______

New Password: ______ Date Changed: ______

New Password: ______ Date Changed: ______

New Password: ______ Date Changed: ______

Security Question Answer 1: ______

Security Question Answer 2: ______

Security Question Answer 3: ______

PASSWORD ORGANIZER

Website Name:

Web Address: ____

Login/Username: ____

Email: ____

Password: ____

New Password: ____ Date Changed: ____

New Password: ____ Date Changed: ____

New Password: ____ Date Changed: ____

Security Question Answer 1: ____

Security Question Answer 2: ____

Security Question Answer 3: ____

Website Name:

Web Address: ____

Login/Username: ____

Email: ____

Password: ____

New Password: ____ Date Changed: ____

New Password: ____ Date Changed: ____

New Password: ____ Date Changed: ____

Security Question Answer 1: ____

Security Question Answer 2: ____

Security Question Answer 3: ____

Website Name:

Web Address: ____

Login/Username: ____

Email: ____

Password: ____

New Password: ____ Date Changed: ____

New Password: ____ Date Changed: ____

New Password: ____ Date Changed: ____

Security Question Answer 1: ____

Security Question Answer 2: ____

Security Question Answer 3: ____

Website Name:

Web Address: ______

Login/Username: ______

Email: ______

Password: ______

New Password: ______ Date Changed: ______

New Password: ______ Date Changed: ______

New Password: ______ Date Changed: ______

Security Question Answer 1: ______

Security Question Answer 2: ______

Security Question Answer 3: ______

Website Name:

Web Address: ______

Login/Username: ______

Email: ______

Password: ______

New Password: ______ Date Changed: ______

New Password: ______ Date Changed: ______

New Password: ______ Date Changed: ______

Security Question Answer 1: ______

Security Question Answer 2: ______

Security Question Answer 3: ______

Website Name:

Web Address: ______

Login/Username: ______

Email: ______

Password: ______

New Password: ______ Date Changed: ______

New Password: ______ Date Changed: ______

New Password: ______ Date Changed: ______

Security Question Answer 1: ______

Security Question Answer 2: ______

Security Question Answer 3: ______

PASSWORD ORGANIZER

Website Name:

Web Address: ____________________
Login/Username: ____________________
Email: ____________________
Password: ____________________
New Password: __________ Date Changed: __________
New Password: __________ Date Changed: __________
New Password: __________ Date Changed: __________
Security Question Answer 1: ____________________
Security Question Answer 2: ____________________
Security Question Answer 3: ____________________

Website Name:

Web Address: ____________________
Login/Username: ____________________
Email: ____________________
Password: ____________________
New Password: __________ Date Changed: __________
New Password: __________ Date Changed: __________
New Password: __________ Date Changed: __________
Security Question Answer 1: ____________________
Security Question Answer 2: ____________________
Security Question Answer 3: ____________________

Website Name:

Web Address: ____________________
Login/Username: ____________________
Email: ____________________
Password: ____________________
New Password: __________ Date Changed: __________
New Password: __________ Date Changed: __________
New Password: __________ Date Changed: __________
Security Question Answer 1: ____________________
Security Question Answer 2: ____________________
Security Question Answer 3: ____________________

PASSWORD ORGANIZER

Website Name:

Web Address: ______

Login/Username: ______

Email: ______

Password: ______

New Password: ______ Date Changed: ______

New Password: ______ Date Changed: ______

New Password: ______ Date Changed: ______

Security Question Answer 1: ______

Security Question Answer 2: ______

Security Question Answer 3: ______

Website Name:

Web Address: ______

Login/Username: ______

Email: ______

Password: ______

New Password: ______ Date Changed: ______

New Password: ______ Date Changed: ______

New Password: ______ Date Changed: ______

Security Question Answer 1: ______

Security Question Answer 2: ______

Security Question Answer 3: ______

Website Name:

Web Address: ______

Login/Username: ______

Email: ______

Password: ______

New Password: ______ Date Changed: ______

New Password: ______ Date Changed: ______

New Password: ______ Date Changed: ______

Security Question Answer 1: ______

Security Question Answer 2: ______

Security Question Answer 3: ______

PASSWORD ORGANIZER

Website Name:

Web Address: ____________________

Login/Username: ____________________

Email: ____________________

Password: ____________________

New Password: ____________________ Date Changed: __________

New Password: ____________________ Date Changed: __________

New Password: ____________________ Date Changed: __________

Security Question Answer 1: ____________________

Security Question Answer 2: ____________________

Security Question Answer 3: ____________________

Website Name:

Web Address: ____________________

Login/Username: ____________________

Email: ____________________

Password: ____________________

New Password: ____________________ Date Changed: __________

New Password: ____________________ Date Changed: __________

New Password: ____________________ Date Changed: __________

Security Question Answer 1: ____________________

Security Question Answer 2: ____________________

Security Question Answer 3: ____________________

Website Name:

Web Address: ____________________

Login/Username: ____________________

Email: ____________________

Password: ____________________

New Password: ____________________ Date Changed: __________

New Password: ____________________ Date Changed: __________

New Password: ____________________ Date Changed: __________

Security Question Answer 1: ____________________

Security Question Answer 2: ____________________

Security Question Answer 3: ____________________

Website Name:

Web Address: ______

Login/Username: ______

Email: ______

Password: ______

New Password: ______ Date Changed: ______

New Password: ______ Date Changed: ______

New Password: ______ Date Changed: ______

Security Question Answer 1: ______

Security Question Answer 2: ______

Security Question Answer 3: ______

Website Name:

Web Address: ______

Login/Username: ______

Email: ______

Password: ______

New Password: ______ Date Changed: ______

New Password: ______ Date Changed: ______

New Password: ______ Date Changed: ______

Security Question Answer 1: ______

Security Question Answer 2: ______

Security Question Answer 3: ______

Website Name:

Web Address: ______

Login/Username: ______

Email: ______

Password: ______

New Password: ______ Date Changed: ______

New Password: ______ Date Changed: ______

New Password: ______ Date Changed: ______

Security Question Answer 1: ______

Security Question Answer 2: ______

Security Question Answer 3: ______

PASSWORD ORGANIZER

Website Name:

Web Address: ______

Login/Username: ______

Email: ______

Password: ______

New Password: ______ Date Changed: ______

New Password: ______ Date Changed: ______

New Password: ______ Date Changed: ______

Security Question Answer 1: ______

Security Question Answer 2: ______

Security Question Answer 3: ______

Website Name:

Web Address: ______

Login/Username: ______

Email: ______

Password: ______

New Password: ______ Date Changed: ______

New Password: ______ Date Changed: ______

New Password: ______ Date Changed: ______

Security Question Answer 1: ______

Security Question Answer 2: ______

Security Question Answer 3: ______

Website Name:

Web Address: ______

Login/Username: ______

Email: ______

Password: ______

New Password: ______ Date Changed: ______

New Password: ______ Date Changed: ______

New Password: ______ Date Changed: ______

Security Question Answer 1: ______

Security Question Answer 2: ______

Security Question Answer 3: ______

Website Name:

Web Address: ____________________

Login/Username: ____________________

Email: ____________________

Password: ____________________

New Password: ____________________ Date Changed: __________

New Password: ____________________ Date Changed: __________

New Password: ____________________ Date Changed: __________

Security Question Answer 1: ____________________

Security Question Answer 2: ____________________

Security Question Answer 3: ____________________

Website Name:

Web Address: ____________________

Login/Username: ____________________

Email: ____________________

Password: ____________________

New Password: ____________________ Date Changed: __________

New Password: ____________________ Date Changed: __________

New Password: ____________________ Date Changed: __________

Security Question Answer 1: ____________________

Security Question Answer 2: ____________________

Security Question Answer 3: ____________________

Website Name:

Web Address: ____________________

Login/Username: ____________________

Email: ____________________

Password: ____________________

New Password: ____________________ Date Changed: __________

New Password: ____________________ Date Changed: __________

New Password: ____________________ Date Changed: __________

Security Question Answer 1: ____________________

Security Question Answer 2: ____________________

Security Question Answer 3: ____________________

PASSWORD ORGANIZER

Website Name:

Web Address: ______

Login/Username: ______

Email: ______

Password: ______

New Password: ______ Date Changed: ______

New Password: ______ Date Changed: ______

New Password: ______ Date Changed: ______

Security Question Answer 1: ______

Security Question Answer 2: ______

Security Question Answer 3: ______

Website Name:

Web Address: ______

Login/Username: ______

Email: ______

Password: ______

New Password: ______ Date Changed: ______

New Password: ______ Date Changed: ______

New Password: ______ Date Changed: ______

Security Question Answer 1: ______

Security Question Answer 2: ______

Security Question Answer 3: ______

Website Name:

Web Address: ______

Login/Username: ______

Email: ______

Password: ______

New Password: ______ Date Changed: ______

New Password: ______ Date Changed: ______

New Password: ______ Date Changed: ______

Security Question Answer 1: ______

Security Question Answer 2: ______

Security Question Answer 3: ______

PASSWORD ORGANIZER

Website Name:

Web Address: ______

Login/Username: ______

Email: ______

Password: ______

New Password: ______ Date Changed: ______

New Password: ______ Date Changed: ______

New Password: ______ Date Changed: ______

Security Question Answer 1: ______

Security Question Answer 2: ______

Security Question Answer 3: ______

Website Name:

Web Address: ______

Login/Username: ______

Email: ______

Password: ______

New Password: ______ Date Changed: ______

New Password: ______ Date Changed: ______

New Password: ______ Date Changed: ______

Security Question Answer 1: ______

Security Question Answer 2: ______

Security Question Answer 3: ______

Website Name:

Web Address: ______

Login/Username: ______

Email: ______

Password: ______

New Password: ______ Date Changed: ______

New Password: ______ Date Changed: ______

New Password: ______ Date Changed: ______

Security Question Answer 1: ______

Security Question Answer 2: ______

Security Question Answer 3: ______

PASSWORD ORGANIZER

Website Name:

Web Address: ______________________

Login/Username: ______________________

Email: ______________________

Password: ______________________

New Password: ______________________ Date Changed: __________

New Password: ______________________ Date Changed: __________

New Password: ______________________ Date Changed: __________

Security Question Answer 1: ______________________

Security Question Answer 2: ______________________

Security Question Answer 3: ______________________

Website Name:

Web Address: ______________________

Login/Username: ______________________

Email: ______________________

Password: ______________________

New Password: ______________________ Date Changed: __________

New Password: ______________________ Date Changed: __________

New Password: ______________________ Date Changed: __________

Security Question Answer 1: ______________________

Security Question Answer 2: ______________________

Security Question Answer 3: ______________________

Website Name:

Web Address: ______________________

Login/Username: ______________________

Email: ______________________

Password: ______________________

New Password: ______________________ Date Changed: __________

New Password: ______________________ Date Changed: __________

New Password: ______________________ Date Changed: __________

Security Question Answer 1: ______________________

Security Question Answer 2: ______________________

Security Question Answer 3: ______________________

Website Name:

Web Address: __________

Login/Username: __________

Email: __________

Password: __________

New Password: __________ Date Changed: __________

New Password: __________ Date Changed: __________

New Password: __________ Date Changed: __________

Security Question Answer 1: __________

Security Question Answer 2: __________

Security Question Answer 3: __________

Website Name:

Web Address: __________

Login/Username: __________

Email: __________

Password: __________

New Password: __________ Date Changed: __________

New Password: __________ Date Changed: __________

New Password: __________ Date Changed: __________

Security Question Answer 1: __________

Security Question Answer 2: __________

Security Question Answer 3: __________

Website Name:

Web Address: __________

Login/Username: __________

Email: __________

Password: __________

New Password: __________ Date Changed: __________

New Password: __________ Date Changed: __________

New Password: __________ Date Changed: __________

Security Question Answer 1: __________

Security Question Answer 2: __________

Security Question Answer 3: __________

PASSWORD ORGANIZER

Website Name:

Web Address: ____________________

Login/Username: ____________________

Email: ____________________

Password: ____________________

New Password: ____________________ Date Changed: __________

New Password: ____________________ Date Changed: __________

New Password: ____________________ Date Changed: __________

Security Question Answer 1: ____________________

Security Question Answer 2: ____________________

Security Question Answer 3: ____________________

Website Name:

Web Address: ____________________

Login/Username: ____________________

Email: ____________________

Password: ____________________

New Password: ____________________ Date Changed: __________

New Password: ____________________ Date Changed: __________

New Password: ____________________ Date Changed: __________

Security Question Answer 1: ____________________

Security Question Answer 2: ____________________

Security Question Answer 3: ____________________

Website Name:

Web Address: ____________________

Login/Username: ____________________

Email: ____________________

Password: ____________________

New Password: ____________________ Date Changed: __________

New Password: ____________________ Date Changed: __________

New Password: ____________________ Date Changed: __________

Security Question Answer 1: ____________________

Security Question Answer 2: ____________________

Security Question Answer 3: ____________________

Website Name:

Web Address: ______________________________

Login/Username: ______________________________

Email: ______________________________

Password: ______________________________

New Password: ____________________ Date Changed: __________

New Password: ____________________ Date Changed: __________

New Password: ____________________ Date Changed: __________

Security Question Answer 1: ______________________________

Security Question Answer 2: ______________________________

Security Question Answer 3: ______________________________

Website Name:

Web Address: ______________________________

Login/Username: ______________________________

Email: ______________________________

Password: ______________________________

New Password: ____________________ Date Changed: __________

New Password: ____________________ Date Changed: __________

New Password: ____________________ Date Changed: __________

Security Question Answer 1: ______________________________

Security Question Answer 2: ______________________________

Security Question Answer 3: ______________________________

Website Name:

Web Address: ______________________________

Login/Username: ______________________________

Email: ______________________________

Password: ______________________________

New Password: ____________________ Date Changed: __________

New Password: ____________________ Date Changed: __________

New Password: ____________________ Date Changed: __________

Security Question Answer 1: ______________________________

Security Question Answer 2: ______________________________

Security Question Answer 3: ______________________________

PASSWORD ORGANIZER

Website Name:

Web Address: ______

Login/Username: ______

Email: ______

Password: ______

New Password: ______ Date Changed: ______

New Password: ______ Date Changed: ______

New Password: ______ Date Changed: ______

Security Question Answer 1: ______

Security Question Answer 2: ______

Security Question Answer 3: ______

Website Name:

Web Address: ______

Login/Username: ______

Email: ______

Password: ______

New Password: ______ Date Changed: ______

New Password: ______ Date Changed: ______

New Password: ______ Date Changed: ______

Security Question Answer 1: ______

Security Question Answer 2: ______

Security Question Answer 3: ______

Website Name:

Web Address: ______

Login/Username: ______

Email: ______

Password: ______

New Password: ______ Date Changed: ______

New Password: ______ Date Changed: ______

New Password: ______ Date Changed: ______

Security Question Answer 1: ______

Security Question Answer 2: ______

Security Question Answer 3: ______

Website Name:

Web Address: __________

Login/Username: __________

Email: __________

Password: __________

New Password: __________ Date Changed: __________

New Password: __________ Date Changed: __________

New Password: __________ Date Changed: __________

Security Question Answer 1: __________

Security Question Answer 2: __________

Security Question Answer 3: __________

Website Name:

Web Address: __________

Login/Username: __________

Email: __________

Password: __________

New Password: __________ Date Changed: __________

New Password: __________ Date Changed: __________

New Password: __________ Date Changed: __________

Security Question Answer 1: __________

Security Question Answer 2: __________

Security Question Answer 3: __________

Website Name:

Web Address: __________

Login/Username: __________

Email: __________

Password: __________

New Password: __________ Date Changed: __________

New Password: __________ Date Changed: __________

New Password: __________ Date Changed: __________

Security Question Answer 1: __________

Security Question Answer 2: __________

Security Question Answer 3: __________

PASSWORD ORGANIZER

Website Name:

Web Address: ____________________

Login/Username: ____________________

Email: ____________________

Password: ____________________

New Password: ____________________ Date Changed: __________

New Password: ____________________ Date Changed: __________

New Password: ____________________ Date Changed: __________

Security Question Answer 1: ____________________

Security Question Answer 2: ____________________

Security Question Answer 3: ____________________

Website Name:

Web Address: ____________________

Login/Username: ____________________

Email: ____________________

Password: ____________________

New Password: ____________________ Date Changed: __________

New Password: ____________________ Date Changed: __________

New Password: ____________________ Date Changed: __________

Security Question Answer 1: ____________________

Security Question Answer 2: ____________________

Security Question Answer 3: ____________________

Website Name:

Web Address: ____________________

Login/Username: ____________________

Email: ____________________

Password: ____________________

New Password: ____________________ Date Changed: __________

New Password: ____________________ Date Changed: __________

New Password: ____________________ Date Changed: __________

Security Question Answer 1: ____________________

Security Question Answer 2: ____________________

Security Question Answer 3: ____________________

Website Name:

Web Address: ____________________
Login/Username: ____________________
Email: ____________________
Password: ____________________
New Password: ____________________ Date Changed: __________
New Password: ____________________ Date Changed: __________
New Password: ____________________ Date Changed: __________
Security Question Answer 1: ____________________
Security Question Answer 2: ____________________
Security Question Answer 3: ____________________

Website Name:

Web Address: ____________________
Login/Username: ____________________
Email: ____________________
Password: ____________________
New Password: ____________________ Date Changed: __________
New Password: ____________________ Date Changed: __________
New Password: ____________________ Date Changed: __________
Security Question Answer 1: ____________________
Security Question Answer 2: ____________________
Security Question Answer 3: ____________________

Website Name:

Web Address: ____________________
Login/Username: ____________________
Email: ____________________
Password: ____________________
New Password: ____________________ Date Changed: __________
New Password: ____________________ Date Changed: __________
New Password: ____________________ Date Changed: __________
Security Question Answer 1: ____________________
Security Question Answer 2: ____________________
Security Question Answer 3: ____________________

PASSWORD ORGANIZER

Website Name:

Web Address: ______

Login/Username: ______

Email: ______

Password: ______

New Password: ______ Date Changed: ______

New Password: ______ Date Changed: ______

New Password: ______ Date Changed: ______

Security Question Answer 1: ______

Security Question Answer 2: ______

Security Question Answer 3: ______

Website Name:

Web Address: ______

Login/Username: ______

Email: ______

Password: ______

New Password: ______ Date Changed: ______

New Password: ______ Date Changed: ______

New Password: ______ Date Changed: ______

Security Question Answer 1: ______

Security Question Answer 2: ______

Security Question Answer 3: ______

Website Name:

Web Address: ______

Login/Username: ______

Email: ______

Password: ______

New Password: ______ Date Changed: ______

New Password: ______ Date Changed: ______

New Password: ______ Date Changed: ______

Security Question Answer 1: ______

Security Question Answer 2: ______

Security Question Answer 3: ______

Website Name:

Web Address: ____________________

Login/Username: ____________________

Email: ____________________

Password: ____________________

New Password: ____________________ Date Changed: __________

New Password: ____________________ Date Changed: __________

New Password: ____________________ Date Changed: __________

Security Question Answer 1: ____________________

Security Question Answer 2: ____________________

Security Question Answer 3: ____________________

Website Name:

Web Address: ____________________

Login/Username: ____________________

Email: ____________________

Password: ____________________

New Password: ____________________ Date Changed: __________

New Password: ____________________ Date Changed: __________

New Password: ____________________ Date Changed: __________

Security Question Answer 1: ____________________

Security Question Answer 2: ____________________

Security Question Answer 3: ____________________

Website Name:

Web Address: ____________________

Login/Username: ____________________

Email: ____________________

Password: ____________________

New Password: ____________________ Date Changed: __________

New Password: ____________________ Date Changed: __________

New Password: ____________________ Date Changed: __________

Security Question Answer 1: ____________________

Security Question Answer 2: ____________________

Security Question Answer 3: ____________________

Website Name:

Web Address: ____________________

Login/Username: ____________________

Email: ____________________

Password: ____________________

New Password: ____________________ Date Changed: __________

New Password: ____________________ Date Changed: __________

New Password: ____________________ Date Changed: __________

Security Question Answer 1: ____________________

Security Question Answer 2: ____________________

Security Question Answer 3: ____________________

Website Name:

Web Address: ____________________

Login/Username: ____________________

Email: ____________________

Password: ____________________

New Password: ____________________ Date Changed: __________

New Password: ____________________ Date Changed: __________

New Password: ____________________ Date Changed: __________

Security Question Answer 1: ____________________

Security Question Answer 2: ____________________

Security Question Answer 3: ____________________

Website Name:

Web Address: ____________________

Login/Username: ____________________

Email: ____________________

Password: ____________________

New Password: ____________________ Date Changed: __________

New Password: ____________________ Date Changed: __________

New Password: ____________________ Date Changed: __________

Security Question Answer 1: ____________________

Security Question Answer 2: ____________________

Security Question Answer 3: ____________________

Website Name:

Web Address: ______

Login/Username: ______

Email: ______

Password: ______

New Password: ______ Date Changed: ______

New Password: ______ Date Changed: ______

New Password: ______ Date Changed: ______

Security Question Answer 1: ______

Security Question Answer 2: ______

Security Question Answer 3: ______

Website Name:

Web Address: ______

Login/Username: ______

Email: ______

Password: ______

New Password: ______ Date Changed: ______

New Password: ______ Date Changed: ______

New Password: ______ Date Changed: ______

Security Question Answer 1: ______

Security Question Answer 2: ______

Security Question Answer 3: ______

Website Name:

Web Address: ______

Login/Username: ______

Email: ______

Password: ______

New Password: ______ Date Changed: ______

New Password: ______ Date Changed: ______

New Password: ______ Date Changed: ______

Security Question Answer 1: ______

Security Question Answer 2: ______

Security Question Answer 3: ______

PASSWORD ORGANIZER

Website Name:

Web Address: ______________________________

Login/Username: ______________________________

Email: ______________________________

Password: ______________________________

New Password: ______________________ Date Changed: __________

New Password: ______________________ Date Changed: __________

New Password: ______________________ Date Changed: __________

Security Question Answer 1: ______________________________

Security Question Answer 2: ______________________________

Security Question Answer 3: ______________________________

Website Name:

Web Address: ______________________________

Login/Username: ______________________________

Email: ______________________________

Password: ______________________________

New Password: ______________________ Date Changed: __________

New Password: ______________________ Date Changed: __________

New Password: ______________________ Date Changed: __________

Security Question Answer 1: ______________________________

Security Question Answer 2: ______________________________

Security Question Answer 3: ______________________________

Website Name:

Web Address: ______________________________

Login/Username: ______________________________

Email: ______________________________

Password: ______________________________

New Password: ______________________ Date Changed: __________

New Password: ______________________ Date Changed: __________

New Password: ______________________ Date Changed: __________

Security Question Answer 1: ______________________________

Security Question Answer 2: ______________________________

Security Question Answer 3: ______________________________

Website Name:

Web Address: ______________________

Login/Username: ______________________

Email: ______________________

Password: ______________________

New Password: ______________ Date Changed: ________

New Password: ______________ Date Changed: ________

New Password: ______________ Date Changed: ________

Security Question Answer 1: ______________________

Security Question Answer 2: ______________________

Security Question Answer 3: ______________________

Website Name:

Web Address: ______________________

Login/Username: ______________________

Email: ______________________

Password: ______________________

New Password: ______________ Date Changed: ________

New Password: ______________ Date Changed: ________

New Password: ______________ Date Changed: ________

Security Question Answer 1: ______________________

Security Question Answer 2: ______________________

Security Question Answer 3: ______________________

Website Name:

Web Address: ______________________

Login/Username: ______________________

Email: ______________________

Password: ______________________

New Password: ______________ Date Changed: ________

New Password: ______________ Date Changed: ________

New Password: ______________ Date Changed: ________

Security Question Answer 1: ______________________

Security Question Answer 2: ______________________

Security Question Answer 3: ______________________

PASSWORD ORGANIZER

Website Name:

Web Address: ____________________

Login/Username: ____________________

Email: ____________________

Password: ____________________

New Password: ____________________ Date Changed: __________

New Password: ____________________ Date Changed: __________

New Password: ____________________ Date Changed: __________

Security Question Answer 1: ____________________

Security Question Answer 2: ____________________

Security Question Answer 3: ____________________

Website Name:

Web Address: ____________________

Login/Username: ____________________

Email: ____________________

Password: ____________________

New Password: ____________________ Date Changed: __________

New Password: ____________________ Date Changed: __________

New Password: ____________________ Date Changed: __________

Security Question Answer 1: ____________________

Security Question Answer 2: ____________________

Security Question Answer 3: ____________________

Website Name:

Web Address: ____________________

Login/Username: ____________________

Email: ____________________

Password: ____________________

New Password: ____________________ Date Changed: __________

New Password: ____________________ Date Changed: __________

New Password: ____________________ Date Changed: __________

Security Question Answer 1: ____________________

Security Question Answer 2: ____________________

Security Question Answer 3: ____________________

Website Name:

Web Address: ____________________

Login/Username: ____________________

Email: ____________________

Password: ____________________

New Password: ____________________ Date Changed: __________

New Password: ____________________ Date Changed: __________

New Password: ____________________ Date Changed: __________

Security Question Answer 1: ____________________

Security Question Answer 2: ____________________

Security Question Answer 3: ____________________

Website Name:

Web Address: ____________________

Login/Username: ____________________

Email: ____________________

Password: ____________________

New Password: ____________________ Date Changed: __________

New Password: ____________________ Date Changed: __________

New Password: ____________________ Date Changed: __________

Security Question Answer 1: ____________________

Security Question Answer 2: ____________________

Security Question Answer 3: ____________________

Website Name:

Web Address: ____________________

Login/Username: ____________________

Email: ____________________

Password: ____________________

New Password: ____________________ Date Changed: __________

New Password: ____________________ Date Changed: __________

New Password: ____________________ Date Changed: __________

Security Question Answer 1: ____________________

Security Question Answer 2: ____________________

Security Question Answer 3: ____________________

PASSWORD ORGANIZER

Website Name:

Web Address: ____________________

Login/Username: ____________________

Email: ____________________

Password: ____________________

New Password: ____________________ Date Changed: __________

New Password: ____________________ Date Changed: __________

New Password: ____________________ Date Changed: __________

Security Question Answer 1: ____________________

Security Question Answer 2: ____________________

Security Question Answer 3: ____________________

Website Name:

Web Address: ____________________

Login/Username: ____________________

Email: ____________________

Password: ____________________

New Password: ____________________ Date Changed: __________

New Password: ____________________ Date Changed: __________

New Password: ____________________ Date Changed: __________

Security Question Answer 1: ____________________

Security Question Answer 2: ____________________

Security Question Answer 3: ____________________

Website Name:

Web Address: ____________________

Login/Username: ____________________

Email: ____________________

Password: ____________________

New Password: ____________________ Date Changed: __________

New Password: ____________________ Date Changed: __________

New Password: ____________________ Date Changed: __________

Security Question Answer 1: ____________________

Security Question Answer 2: ____________________

Security Question Answer 3: ____________________

PASSWORD ORGANIZER

Website Name:

Web Address: ______________________

Login/Username: ______________________

Email: ______________________

Password: ______________________

New Password: ______________________ Date Changed: __________

New Password: ______________________ Date Changed: __________

New Password: ______________________ Date Changed: __________

Security Question Answer 1: ______________________

Security Question Answer 2: ______________________

Security Question Answer 3: ______________________

Website Name:

Web Address: ______________________

Login/Username: ______________________

Email: ______________________

Password: ______________________

New Password: ______________________ Date Changed: __________

New Password: ______________________ Date Changed: __________

New Password: ______________________ Date Changed: __________

Security Question Answer 1: ______________________

Security Question Answer 2: ______________________

Security Question Answer 3: ______________________

Website Name:

Web Address: ______________________

Login/Username: ______________________

Email: ______________________

Password: ______________________

New Password: ______________________ Date Changed: __________

New Password: ______________________ Date Changed: __________

New Password: ______________________ Date Changed: __________

Security Question Answer 1: ______________________

Security Question Answer 2: ______________________

Security Question Answer 3: ______________________

PASSWORD ORGANIZER

Website Name:

Web Address: ______
Login/Username: ______
Email: ______
Password: ______
New Password: ______ Date Changed: ______
New Password: ______ Date Changed: ______
New Password: ______ Date Changed: ______
Security Question Answer 1: ______
Security Question Answer 2: ______
Security Question Answer 3: ______

Website Name:

Web Address: ______
Login/Username: ______
Email: ______
Password: ______
New Password: ______ Date Changed: ______
New Password: ______ Date Changed: ______
New Password: ______ Date Changed: ______
Security Question Answer 1: ______
Security Question Answer 2: ______
Security Question Answer 3: ______

Website Name:

Web Address: ______
Login/Username: ______
Email: ______
Password: ______
New Password: ______ Date Changed: ______
New Password: ______ Date Changed: ______
New Password: ______ Date Changed: ______
Security Question Answer 1: ______
Security Question Answer 2: ______
Security Question Answer 3: ______

Website Name:

Web Address: ____________________

Login/Username: ____________________

Email: ____________________

Password: ____________________

New Password: ____________________ Date Changed: __________

New Password: ____________________ Date Changed: __________

New Password: ____________________ Date Changed: __________

Security Question Answer 1: ____________________

Security Question Answer 2: ____________________

Security Question Answer 3: ____________________

Website Name:

Web Address: ____________________

Login/Username: ____________________

Email: ____________________

Password: ____________________

New Password: ____________________ Date Changed: __________

New Password: ____________________ Date Changed: __________

New Password: ____________________ Date Changed: __________

Security Question Answer 1: ____________________

Security Question Answer 2: ____________________

Security Question Answer 3: ____________________

Website Name:

Web Address: ____________________

Login/Username: ____________________

Email: ____________________

Password: ____________________

New Password: ____________________ Date Changed: __________

New Password: ____________________ Date Changed: __________

New Password: ____________________ Date Changed: __________

Security Question Answer 1: ____________________

Security Question Answer 2: ____________________

Security Question Answer 3: ____________________

PASSWORD ORGANIZER

Website Name:

Web Address: ______

Login/Username: ______

Email: ______

Password: ______

New Password: ______ Date Changed: ______

New Password: ______ Date Changed: ______

New Password: ______ Date Changed: ______

Security Question Answer 1: ______

Security Question Answer 2: ______

Security Question Answer 3: ______

Website Name:

Web Address: ______

Login/Username: ______

Email: ______

Password: ______

New Password: ______ Date Changed: ______

New Password: ______ Date Changed: ______

New Password: ______ Date Changed: ______

Security Question Answer 1: ______

Security Question Answer 2: ______

Security Question Answer 3: ______

Website Name:

Web Address: ______

Login/Username: ______

Email: ______

Password: ______

New Password: ______ Date Changed: ______

New Password: ______ Date Changed: ______

New Password: ______ Date Changed: ______

Security Question Answer 1: ______

Security Question Answer 2: ______

Security Question Answer 3: ______

Website Name:

Web Address: ______________________________

Login/Username: ______________________________

Email: ______________________________

Password: ______________________________

New Password: ____________________ Date Changed: __________

New Password: ____________________ Date Changed: __________

New Password: ____________________ Date Changed: __________

Security Question Answer 1: ______________________________

Security Question Answer 2: ______________________________

Security Question Answer 3: ______________________________

Website Name:

Web Address: ______________________________

Login/Username: ______________________________

Email: ______________________________

Password: ______________________________

New Password: ____________________ Date Changed: __________

New Password: ____________________ Date Changed: __________

New Password: ____________________ Date Changed: __________

Security Question Answer 1: ______________________________

Security Question Answer 2: ______________________________

Security Question Answer 3: ______________________________

Website Name:

Web Address: ______________________________

Login/Username: ______________________________

Email: ______________________________

Password: ______________________________

New Password: ____________________ Date Changed: __________

New Password: ____________________ Date Changed: __________

New Password: ____________________ Date Changed: __________

Security Question Answer 1: ______________________________

Security Question Answer 2: ______________________________

Security Question Answer 3: ______________________________

PASSWORD ORGANIZER

Website Name:

Web Address: ____________________

Login/Username: ____________________

Email: ____________________

Password: ____________________

New Password: ____________________ Date Changed: __________

New Password: ____________________ Date Changed: __________

New Password: ____________________ Date Changed: __________

Security Question Answer 1: ____________________

Security Question Answer 2: ____________________

Security Question Answer 3: ____________________

Website Name:

Web Address: ____________________

Login/Username: ____________________

Email: ____________________

Password: ____________________

New Password: ____________________ Date Changed: __________

New Password: ____________________ Date Changed: __________

New Password: ____________________ Date Changed: __________

Security Question Answer 1: ____________________

Security Question Answer 2: ____________________

Security Question Answer 3: ____________________

Website Name:

Web Address: ____________________

Login/Username: ____________________

Email: ____________________

Password: ____________________

New Password: ____________________ Date Changed: __________

New Password: ____________________ Date Changed: __________

New Password: ____________________ Date Changed: __________

Security Question Answer 1: ____________________

Security Question Answer 2: ____________________

Security Question Answer 3: ____________________

Website Name:

Web Address: ______

Login/Username: ______

Email: ______

Password: ______

New Password: ______ Date Changed: ______

New Password: ______ Date Changed: ______

New Password: ______ Date Changed: ______

Security Question Answer 1: ______

Security Question Answer 2: ______

Security Question Answer 3: ______

Website Name:

Web Address: ______

Login/Username: ______

Email: ______

Password: ______

New Password: ______ Date Changed: ______

New Password: ______ Date Changed: ______

New Password: ______ Date Changed: ______

Security Question Answer 1: ______

Security Question Answer 2: ______

Security Question Answer 3: ______

Website Name:

Web Address: ______

Login/Username: ______

Email: ______

Password: ______

New Password: ______ Date Changed: ______

New Password: ______ Date Changed: ______

New Password: ______ Date Changed: ______

Security Question Answer 1: ______

Security Question Answer 2: ______

Security Question Answer 3: ______

PASSWORD ORGANIZER

Website Name:

Web Address: ______________________________

Login/Username: ______________________________

Email: ______________________________

Password: ______________________________

New Password: ____________________ Date Changed: __________

New Password: ____________________ Date Changed: __________

New Password: ____________________ Date Changed: __________

Security Question Answer 1: ______________________________

Security Question Answer 2: ______________________________

Security Question Answer 3: ______________________________

Website Name:

Web Address: ______________________________

Login/Username: ______________________________

Email: ______________________________

Password: ______________________________

New Password: ____________________ Date Changed: __________

New Password: ____________________ Date Changed: __________

New Password: ____________________ Date Changed: __________

Security Question Answer 1: ______________________________

Security Question Answer 2: ______________________________

Security Question Answer 3: ______________________________

Website Name:

Web Address: ______________________________

Login/Username: ______________________________

Email: ______________________________

Password: ______________________________

New Password: ____________________ Date Changed: __________

New Password: ____________________ Date Changed: __________

New Password: ____________________ Date Changed: __________

Security Question Answer 1: ______________________________

Security Question Answer 2: ______________________________

Security Question Answer 3: ______________________________

Website Name:

Web Address: ______

Login/Username: ______

Email: ______

Password: ______

New Password: ______ Date Changed: ______

New Password: ______ Date Changed: ______

New Password: ______ Date Changed: ______

Security Question Answer 1: ______

Security Question Answer 2: ______

Security Question Answer 3: ______

Website Name:

Web Address: ______

Login/Username: ______

Email: ______

Password: ______

New Password: ______ Date Changed: ______

New Password: ______ Date Changed: ______

New Password: ______ Date Changed: ______

Security Question Answer 1: ______

Security Question Answer 2: ______

Security Question Answer 3: ______

Website Name:

Web Address: ______

Login/Username: ______

Email: ______

Password: ______

New Password: ______ Date Changed: ______

New Password: ______ Date Changed: ______

New Password: ______ Date Changed: ______

Security Question Answer 1: ______

Security Question Answer 2: ______

Security Question Answer 3: ______

PASSWORD ORGANIZER

Website Name:

Web Address: ______

Login/Username: ______

Email: ______

Password: ______

New Password: ______ Date Changed: ______

New Password: ______ Date Changed: ______

New Password: ______ Date Changed: ______

Security Question Answer 1: ______

Security Question Answer 2: ______

Security Question Answer 3: ______

Website Name:

Web Address: ______

Login/Username: ______

Email: ______

Password: ______

New Password: ______ Date Changed: ______

New Password: ______ Date Changed: ______

New Password: ______ Date Changed: ______

Security Question Answer 1: ______

Security Question Answer 2: ______

Security Question Answer 3: ______

Website Name:

Web Address: ______

Login/Username: ______

Email: ______

Password: ______

New Password: ______ Date Changed: ______

New Password: ______ Date Changed: ______

New Password: ______ Date Changed: ______

Security Question Answer 1: ______

Security Question Answer 2: ______

Security Question Answer 3: ______

Website Name:

Web Address: __________

Login/Username: __________

Email: __________

Password: __________

New Password: __________ Date Changed: __________

New Password: __________ Date Changed: __________

New Password: __________ Date Changed: __________

Security Question Answer 1: __________

Security Question Answer 2: __________

Security Question Answer 3: __________

Website Name:

Web Address: __________

Login/Username: __________

Email: __________

Password: __________

New Password: __________ Date Changed: __________

New Password: __________ Date Changed: __________

New Password: __________ Date Changed: __________

Security Question Answer 1: __________

Security Question Answer 2: __________

Security Question Answer 3: __________

Website Name:

Web Address: __________

Login/Username: __________

Email: __________

Password: __________

New Password: __________ Date Changed: __________

New Password: __________ Date Changed: __________

New Password: __________ Date Changed: __________

Security Question Answer 1: __________

Security Question Answer 2: __________

Security Question Answer 3: __________

PASSWORD ORGANIZER

Website Name:

Web Address: ______
Login/Username: ______
Email: ______
Password: ______
New Password: ______ Date Changed: ______
New Password: ______ Date Changed: ______
New Password: ______ Date Changed: ______
Security Question Answer 1: ______
Security Question Answer 2: ______
Security Question Answer 3: ______

Website Name:

Web Address: ______
Login/Username: ______
Email: ______
Password: ______
New Password: ______ Date Changed: ______
New Password: ______ Date Changed: ______
New Password: ______ Date Changed: ______
Security Question Answer 1: ______
Security Question Answer 2: ______
Security Question Answer 3: ______

Website Name:

Web Address: ______
Login/Username: ______
Email: ______
Password: ______
New Password: ______ Date Changed: ______
New Password: ______ Date Changed: ______
New Password: ______ Date Changed: ______
Security Question Answer 1: ______
Security Question Answer 2: ______
Security Question Answer 3: ______

Website Name:

Web Address: ______

Login/Username: ______

Email: ______

Password: ______

New Password: ______ Date Changed: ______

New Password: ______ Date Changed: ______

New Password: ______ Date Changed: ______

Security Question Answer 1: ______

Security Question Answer 2: ______

Security Question Answer 3: ______

Website Name:

Web Address: ______

Login/Username: ______

Email: ______

Password: ______

New Password: ______ Date Changed: ______

New Password: ______ Date Changed: ______

New Password: ______ Date Changed: ______

Security Question Answer 1: ______

Security Question Answer 2: ______

Security Question Answer 3: ______

Website Name:

Web Address: ______

Login/Username: ______

Email: ______

Password: ______

New Password: ______ Date Changed: ______

New Password: ______ Date Changed: ______

New Password: ______ Date Changed: ______

Security Question Answer 1: ______

Security Question Answer 2: ______

Security Question Answer 3: ______

PASSWORD ORGANIZER

Website Name:

Web Address: ____________________

Login/Username: ____________________

Email: ____________________

Password: ____________________

New Password: ____________________ Date Changed: ____________

New Password: ____________________ Date Changed: ____________

New Password: ____________________ Date Changed: ____________

Security Question Answer 1: ____________________

Security Question Answer 2: ____________________

Security Question Answer 3: ____________________

Website Name:

Web Address: ____________________

Login/Username: ____________________

Email: ____________________

Password: ____________________

New Password: ____________________ Date Changed: ____________

New Password: ____________________ Date Changed: ____________

New Password: ____________________ Date Changed: ____________

Security Question Answer 1: ____________________

Security Question Answer 2: ____________________

Security Question Answer 3: ____________________

Website Name:

Web Address: ____________________

Login/Username: ____________________

Email: ____________________

Password: ____________________

New Password: ____________________ Date Changed: ____________

New Password: ____________________ Date Changed: ____________

New Password: ____________________ Date Changed: ____________

Security Question Answer 1: ____________________

Security Question Answer 2: ____________________

Security Question Answer 3: ____________________

Website Name:

Web Address: ______

Login/Username: ______

Email: ______

Password: ______

New Password: ______ Date Changed: ______

New Password: ______ Date Changed: ______

New Password: ______ Date Changed: ______

Security Question Answer 1: ______

Security Question Answer 2: ______

Security Question Answer 3: ______

Website Name:

Web Address: ______

Login/Username: ______

Email: ______

Password: ______

New Password: ______ Date Changed: ______

New Password: ______ Date Changed: ______

New Password: ______ Date Changed: ______

Security Question Answer 1: ______

Security Question Answer 2: ______

Security Question Answer 3: ______

Website Name:

Web Address: ______

Login/Username: ______

Email: ______

Password: ______

New Password: ______ Date Changed: ______

New Password: ______ Date Changed: ______

New Password: ______ Date Changed: ______

Security Question Answer 1: ______

Security Question Answer 2: ______

Security Question Answer 3: ______

PASSWORD ORGANIZER

Website Name:

Web Address: ______

Login/Username: ______

Email: ______

Password: ______

New Password: ______ Date Changed: ______

New Password: ______ Date Changed: ______

New Password: ______ Date Changed: ______

Security Question Answer 1: ______

Security Question Answer 2: ______

Security Question Answer 3: ______

Website Name:

Web Address: ______

Login/Username: ______

Email: ______

Password: ______

New Password: ______ Date Changed: ______

New Password: ______ Date Changed: ______

New Password: ______ Date Changed: ______

Security Question Answer 1: ______

Security Question Answer 2: ______

Security Question Answer 3: ______

Website Name:

Web Address: ______

Login/Username: ______

Email: ______

Password: ______

New Password: ______ Date Changed: ______

New Password: ______ Date Changed: ______

New Password: ______ Date Changed: ______

Security Question Answer 1: ______

Security Question Answer 2: ______

Security Question Answer 3: ______

Website Name:

Web Address: __________
Login/Username: __________
Email: __________
Password: __________
New Password: __________ Date Changed: __________
New Password: __________ Date Changed: __________
New Password: __________ Date Changed: __________
Security Question Answer 1: __________
Security Question Answer 2: __________
Security Question Answer 3: __________

Website Name:

Web Address: __________
Login/Username: __________
Email: __________
Password: __________
New Password: __________ Date Changed: __________
New Password: __________ Date Changed: __________
New Password: __________ Date Changed: __________
Security Question Answer 1: __________
Security Question Answer 2: __________
Security Question Answer 3: __________

Website Name:

Web Address: __________
Login/Username: __________
Email: __________
Password: __________
New Password: __________ Date Changed: __________
New Password: __________ Date Changed: __________
New Password: __________ Date Changed: __________
Security Question Answer 1: __________
Security Question Answer 2: __________
Security Question Answer 3: __________

PASSWORD ORGANIZER

Website Name:

Web Address: ______

Login/Username: ______

Email: ______

Password: ______

New Password: ______ Date Changed: ______

New Password: ______ Date Changed: ______

New Password: ______ Date Changed: ______

Security Question Answer 1: ______

Security Question Answer 2: ______

Security Question Answer 3: ______

Website Name:

Web Address: ______

Login/Username: ______

Email: ______

Password: ______

New Password: ______ Date Changed: ______

New Password: ______ Date Changed: ______

New Password: ______ Date Changed: ______

Security Question Answer 1: ______

Security Question Answer 2: ______

Security Question Answer 3: ______

Website Name:

Web Address: ______

Login/Username: ______

Email: ______

Password: ______

New Password: ______ Date Changed: ______

New Password: ______ Date Changed: ______

New Password: ______ Date Changed: ______

Security Question Answer 1: ______

Security Question Answer 2: ______

Security Question Answer 3: ______

PASSWORD ORGANIZER

W

Website Name:

Web Address: __________
Login/Username: __________
Email: __________
Password: __________
New Password: __________ Date Changed: __________
New Password: __________ Date Changed: __________
New Password: __________ Date Changed: __________
Security Question Answer 1: __________
Security Question Answer 2: __________
Security Question Answer 3: __________

Website Name:

Web Address: __________
Login/Username: __________
Email: __________
Password: __________
New Password: __________ Date Changed: __________
New Password: __________ Date Changed: __________
New Password: __________ Date Changed: __________
Security Question Answer 1: __________
Security Question Answer 2: __________
Security Question Answer 3: __________

Website Name:

Web Address: __________
Login/Username: __________
Email: __________
Password: __________
New Password: __________ Date Changed: __________
New Password: __________ Date Changed: __________
New Password: __________ Date Changed: __________
Security Question Answer 1: __________
Security Question Answer 2: __________
Security Question Answer 3: __________

PASSWORD ORGANIZER

Website Name:

Web Address: ______________________________

Login/Username: ______________________________

Email: ______________________________

Password: ______________________________

New Password: ____________________ Date Changed: __________

New Password: ____________________ Date Changed: __________

New Password: ____________________ Date Changed: __________

Security Question Answer 1: ______________________________

Security Question Answer 2: ______________________________

Security Question Answer 3: ______________________________

Website Name:

Web Address: ______________________________

Login/Username: ______________________________

Email: ______________________________

Password: ______________________________

New Password: ____________________ Date Changed: __________

New Password: ____________________ Date Changed: __________

New Password: ____________________ Date Changed: __________

Security Question Answer 1: ______________________________

Security Question Answer 2: ______________________________

Security Question Answer 3: ______________________________

Website Name:

Web Address: ______________________________

Login/Username: ______________________________

Email: ______________________________

Password: ______________________________

New Password: ____________________ Date Changed: __________

New Password: ____________________ Date Changed: __________

New Password: ____________________ Date Changed: __________

Security Question Answer 1: ______________________________

Security Question Answer 2: ______________________________

Security Question Answer 3: ______________________________

Website Name:

Web Address: ______________________

Login/Username: ______________________

Email: ______________________

Password: ______________________

New Password: ______________________ Date Changed: __________

New Password: ______________________ Date Changed: __________

New Password: ______________________ Date Changed: __________

Security Question Answer 1: ______________________

Security Question Answer 2: ______________________

Security Question Answer 3: ______________________

Website Name:

Web Address: ______________________

Login/Username: ______________________

Email: ______________________

Password: ______________________

New Password: ______________________ Date Changed: __________

New Password: ______________________ Date Changed: __________

New Password: ______________________ Date Changed: __________

Security Question Answer 1: ______________________

Security Question Answer 2: ______________________

Security Question Answer 3: ______________________

Website Name:

Web Address: ______________________

Login/Username: ______________________

Email: ______________________

Password: ______________________

New Password: ______________________ Date Changed: __________

New Password: ______________________ Date Changed: __________

New Password: ______________________ Date Changed: __________

Security Question Answer 1: ______________________

Security Question Answer 2: ______________________

Security Question Answer 3: ______________________

PASSWORD ORGANIZER

Website Name:

Web Address: ____________________
Login/Username: ____________________
Email: ____________________
Password: ____________________
New Password: ____________________ Date Changed: __________
New Password: ____________________ Date Changed: __________
New Password: ____________________ Date Changed: __________
Security Question Answer 1: ____________________
Security Question Answer 2: ____________________
Security Question Answer 3: ____________________

Website Name:

Web Address: ____________________
Login/Username: ____________________
Email: ____________________
Password: ____________________
New Password: ____________________ Date Changed: __________
New Password: ____________________ Date Changed: __________
New Password: ____________________ Date Changed: __________
Security Question Answer 1: ____________________
Security Question Answer 2: ____________________
Security Question Answer 3: ____________________

Website Name:

Web Address: ____________________
Login/Username: ____________________
Email: ____________________
Password: ____________________
New Password: ____________________ Date Changed: __________
New Password: ____________________ Date Changed: __________
New Password: ____________________ Date Changed: __________
Security Question Answer 1: ____________________
Security Question Answer 2: ____________________
Security Question Answer 3: ____________________

Website Name:

Web Address: ____________________

Login/Username: ____________________

Email: ____________________

Password: ____________________

New Password: ____________________ Date Changed: __________

New Password: ____________________ Date Changed: __________

New Password: ____________________ Date Changed: __________

Security Question Answer 1: ____________________

Security Question Answer 2: ____________________

Security Question Answer 3: ____________________

Website Name:

Web Address: ____________________

Login/Username: ____________________

Email: ____________________

Password: ____________________

New Password: ____________________ Date Changed: __________

New Password: ____________________ Date Changed: __________

New Password: ____________________ Date Changed: __________

Security Question Answer 1: ____________________

Security Question Answer 2: ____________________

Security Question Answer 3: ____________________

Website Name:

Web Address: ____________________

Login/Username: ____________________

Email: ____________________

Password: ____________________

New Password: ____________________ Date Changed: __________

New Password: ____________________ Date Changed: __________

New Password: ____________________ Date Changed: __________

Security Question Answer 1: ____________________

Security Question Answer 2: ____________________

Security Question Answer 3: ____________________

PASSWORD ORGANIZER

Website Name:

Web Address: ____________________

Login/Username: ____________________

Email: ____________________

Password: ____________________

New Password: ____________________ Date Changed: __________

New Password: ____________________ Date Changed: __________

New Password: ____________________ Date Changed: __________

Security Question Answer 1: ____________________

Security Question Answer 2: ____________________

Security Question Answer 3: ____________________

Website Name:

Web Address: ____________________

Login/Username: ____________________

Email: ____________________

Password: ____________________

New Password: ____________________ Date Changed: __________

New Password: ____________________ Date Changed: __________

New Password: ____________________ Date Changed: __________

Security Question Answer 1: ____________________

Security Question Answer 2: ____________________

Security Question Answer 3: ____________________

Website Name:

Web Address: ____________________

Login/Username: ____________________

Email: ____________________

Password: ____________________

New Password: ____________________ Date Changed: __________

New Password: ____________________ Date Changed: __________

New Password: ____________________ Date Changed: __________

Security Question Answer 1: ____________________

Security Question Answer 2: ____________________

Security Question Answer 3: ____________________

Website Name:

Web Address: ______

Login/Username: ______

Email: ______

Password: ______

New Password: ______ Date Changed: ______

New Password: ______ Date Changed: ______

New Password: ______ Date Changed: ______

Security Question Answer 1: ______

Security Question Answer 2: ______

Security Question Answer 3: ______

Website Name:

Web Address: ______

Login/Username: ______

Email: ______

Password: ______

New Password: ______ Date Changed: ______

New Password: ______ Date Changed: ______

New Password: ______ Date Changed: ______

Security Question Answer 1: ______

Security Question Answer 2: ______

Security Question Answer 3: ______

Website Name:

Web Address: ______

Login/Username: ______

Email: ______

Password: ______

New Password: ______ Date Changed: ______

New Password: ______ Date Changed: ______

New Password: ______ Date Changed: ______

Security Question Answer 1: ______

Security Question Answer 2: ______

Security Question Answer 3: ______

PASSWORD ORGANIZER

Website Name:

Web Address: ____________________

Login/Username: ____________________

Email: ____________________

Password: ____________________

New Password: ____________________ Date Changed: __________

New Password: ____________________ Date Changed: __________

New Password: ____________________ Date Changed: __________

Security Question Answer 1: ____________________

Security Question Answer 2: ____________________

Security Question Answer 3: ____________________

Website Name:

Web Address: ____________________

Login/Username: ____________________

Email: ____________________

Password: ____________________

New Password: ____________________ Date Changed: __________

New Password: ____________________ Date Changed: __________

New Password: ____________________ Date Changed: __________

Security Question Answer 1: ____________________

Security Question Answer 2: ____________________

Security Question Answer 3: ____________________

Website Name:

Web Address: ____________________

Login/Username: ____________________

Email: ____________________

Password: ____________________

New Password: ____________________ Date Changed: __________

New Password: ____________________ Date Changed: __________

New Password: ____________________ Date Changed: __________

Security Question Answer 1: ____________________

Security Question Answer 2: ____________________

Security Question Answer 3: ____________________

Website Name:

Web Address: ____________________

Login/Username: ____________________

Email: ____________________

Password: ____________________

New Password: ____________ Date Changed: ______

New Password: ____________ Date Changed: ______

New Password: ____________ Date Changed: ______

Security Question Answer 1: ____________________

Security Question Answer 2: ____________________

Security Question Answer 3: ____________________

Website Name:

Web Address: ____________________

Login/Username: ____________________

Email: ____________________

Password: ____________________

New Password: ____________ Date Changed: ______

New Password: ____________ Date Changed: ______

New Password: ____________ Date Changed: ______

Security Question Answer 1: ____________________

Security Question Answer 2: ____________________

Security Question Answer 3: ____________________

Website Name:

Web Address: ____________________

Login/Username: ____________________

Email: ____________________

Password: ____________________

New Password: ____________ Date Changed: ______

New Password: ____________ Date Changed: ______

New Password: ____________ Date Changed: ______

Security Question Answer 1: ____________________

Security Question Answer 2: ____________________

Security Question Answer 3: ____________________

PASSWORD ORGANIZER

Website Name:

Web Address: ______________________

Login/Username: ______________________

Email: ______________________

Password: ______________________

New Password: ______________________ Date Changed: __________

New Password: ______________________ Date Changed: __________

New Password: ______________________ Date Changed: __________

Security Question Answer 1: ______________________

Security Question Answer 2: ______________________

Security Question Answer 3: ______________________

Website Name:

Web Address: ______________________

Login/Username: ______________________

Email: ______________________

Password: ______________________

New Password: ______________________ Date Changed: __________

New Password: ______________________ Date Changed: __________

New Password: ______________________ Date Changed: __________

Security Question Answer 1: ______________________

Security Question Answer 2: ______________________

Security Question Answer 3: ______________________

Website Name:

Web Address: ______________________

Login/Username: ______________________

Email: ______________________

Password: ______________________

New Password: ______________________ Date Changed: __________

New Password: ______________________ Date Changed: __________

New Password: ______________________ Date Changed: __________

Security Question Answer 1: ______________________

Security Question Answer 2: ______________________

Security Question Answer 3: ______________________

Website Name:

Web Address: ______

Login/Username: ______

Email: ______

Password: ______

New Password: ______ Date Changed: ______

New Password: ______ Date Changed: ______

New Password: ______ Date Changed: ______

Security Question Answer 1: ______

Security Question Answer 2: ______

Security Question Answer 3: ______

Website Name:

Web Address: ______

Login/Username: ______

Email: ______

Password: ______

New Password: ______ Date Changed: ______

New Password: ______ Date Changed: ______

New Password: ______ Date Changed: ______

Security Question Answer 1: ______

Security Question Answer 2: ______

Security Question Answer 3: ______

Website Name:

Web Address: ______

Login/Username: ______

Email: ______

Password: ______

New Password: ______ Date Changed: ______

New Password: ______ Date Changed: ______

New Password: ______ Date Changed: ______

Security Question Answer 1: ______

Security Question Answer 2: ______

Security Question Answer 3: ______

PASSWORD ORGANIZER

Website Name:

Web Address: ______________________________
Login/Username: ______________________________
Email: ______________________________
Password: ______________________________
New Password: ____________________ Date Changed: __________
New Password: ____________________ Date Changed: __________
New Password: ____________________ Date Changed: __________
Security Question Answer 1: ______________________________
Security Question Answer 2: ______________________________
Security Question Answer 3: ______________________________

Website Name:

Web Address: ______________________________
Login/Username: ______________________________
Email: ______________________________
Password: ______________________________
New Password: ____________________ Date Changed: __________
New Password: ____________________ Date Changed: __________
New Password: ____________________ Date Changed: __________
Security Question Answer 1: ______________________________
Security Question Answer 2: ______________________________
Security Question Answer 3: ______________________________

Website Name:

Web Address: ______________________________
Login/Username: ______________________________
Email: ______________________________
Password: ______________________________
New Password: ____________________ Date Changed: __________
New Password: ____________________ Date Changed: __________
New Password: ____________________ Date Changed: __________
Security Question Answer 1: ______________________________
Security Question Answer 2: ______________________________
Security Question Answer 3: ______________________________

Website Name:

Web Address: ______

Login/Username: ______

Email: ______

Password: ______

New Password: ______ Date Changed: ______

New Password: ______ Date Changed: ______

New Password: ______ Date Changed: ______

Security Question Answer 1: ______

Security Question Answer 2: ______

Security Question Answer 3: ______

Website Name:

Web Address: ______

Login/Username: ______

Email: ______

Password: ______

New Password: ______ Date Changed: ______

New Password: ______ Date Changed: ______

New Password: ______ Date Changed: ______

Security Question Answer 1: ______

Security Question Answer 2: ______

Security Question Answer 3: ______

Website Name:

Web Address: ______

Login/Username: ______

Email: ______

Password: ______

New Password: ______ Date Changed: ______

New Password: ______ Date Changed: ______

New Password: ______ Date Changed: ______

Security Question Answer 1: ______

Security Question Answer 2: ______

Security Question Answer 3: ______

PASSWORD ORGANIZER

Website Name:

Web Address: ______

Login/Username: ______

Email: ______

Password: ______

New Password: ______ Date Changed: ______

New Password: ______ Date Changed: ______

New Password: ______ Date Changed: ______

Security Question Answer 1: ______

Security Question Answer 2: ______

Security Question Answer 3: ______

Website Name:

Web Address: ______

Login/Username: ______

Email: ______

Password: ______

New Password: ______ Date Changed: ______

New Password: ______ Date Changed: ______

New Password: ______ Date Changed: ______

Security Question Answer 1: ______

Security Question Answer 2: ______

Security Question Answer 3: ______

Website Name:

Web Address: ______

Login/Username: ______

Email: ______

Password: ______

New Password: ______ Date Changed: ______

New Password: ______ Date Changed: ______

New Password: ______ Date Changed: ______

Security Question Answer 1: ______

Security Question Answer 2: ______

Security Question Answer 3: ______

Website Name:

Web Address: ______

Login/Username: ______

Email: ______

Password: ______

New Password: ______ Date Changed: ______

New Password: ______ Date Changed: ______

New Password: ______ Date Changed: ______

Security Question Answer 1: ______

Security Question Answer 2: ______

Security Question Answer 3: ______

Website Name:

Web Address: ______

Login/Username: ______

Email: ______

Password: ______

New Password: ______ Date Changed: ______

New Password: ______ Date Changed: ______

New Password: ______ Date Changed: ______

Security Question Answer 1: ______

Security Question Answer 2: ______

Security Question Answer 3: ______

Website Name:

Web Address: ______

Login/Username: ______

Email: ______

Password: ______

New Password: ______ Date Changed: ______

New Password: ______ Date Changed: ______

New Password: ______ Date Changed: ______

Security Question Answer 1: ______

Security Question Answer 2: ______

Security Question Answer 3: ______

PASSWORD ORGANIZER

Thank You

For Your Purchase!

We love to hear your feedback.
If you liked our Password Organizer
please let us know and leave
a review on Amazon.

Find more of our fun and useful
life journals at:

www.hometreespress.com

HomeTrees Press
Ojai • California

Made in the USA
Monee, IL
04 November 2026

67377499R00059